A NEW BIOLOGY
OF RELIGION

A NEW BIOLOGY OF RELIGION

Spiritual Practice and the Life of the Body

Michael Steinberg

BLUE DISTANCE PRESS

ROCHESTER, NEW YORK

This is an unaltered reprint
of a book published in 2012
in hardcover and e-book
by Praeger, an imprint of ABC-Clio.
Copyright 2012 Michael Steinberg
First paperback edition 2014
ISBN-13: 978-0692204238
ISBN-10: 0692204237
Cover illustration by Kahn/Selesnick
www.kahnselesnick.com

for my parents

Contents

Preface and Acknowledgments

Among Hindus it is traditional to begin books with an invocation to Ganesh, the elephant-headed lord of beginnings and remover of obstacles. This is not just true of books. Every serious undertaking, be it a ritual, a construction project, a concert, a dance, or a journey, is best begun by propitiating him. Authors, though, have a special tie to the god, because he himself is said to be a scribe. The sage Vyasa engaged him to transcribe the great epic poem of the *Mahabharata*, and according to some stories, Ganesh broke off one of his tusks to use as a pen so he could keep up with the recitation.

Writing is often tedious and frustrating, obstructed as much by misleading fluency as it is by writer's block. One can easily see why a remover of obstacles would be a useful ally. But there are deeper reasons for Ganesh to stand at the start of every book. He does not merely place himself at beginnings. He is found at entryways, too. Indeed, he was created by his mother Parvati to guard the door while she bathed, and ever since then he has watched over the gates of homes, temples, and palaces.

Beginnings and doorways: Ganesh stands at the point where two spaces, two forms of experience, two worlds, meet—where people pass from one realm to another. Part human and part animal, fond of sweets and a great dancer, lazy but the captain of Shiva's mutant army of ganas (hence another of his names, "Ganapathi" or "Lord of hosts"), he is Hinduism's emblem of the liminal, the in-between state. Ganesh is an agent of change. He is the doorman who ushers you into the presence of something else.

That, after all, is what should happen when you enter the sacred space of a Hindu temple or the charged time of a ritual. And it should happen, too, when you open a book and begin reading. Only fairy tales start with "Once upon a time," but every book that does more than convey information should slip the reader into a time and an environment different from the one that rushes back in when the covers close or the e-reader turns off.

Writers and books alike live in a liminal world, the space between reality and possibility, perhaps, or the space between what we take for reality and reality itself. Some people write to find their way back to the world of their readers. Others write as a way to spend some time out of that world, and they hope to draw their readers out of it, too. In either case, it is a matter of creating passages through the liminal and the in-between, the realm that Ganesh helps us enter.

This book is no exception. If anything, it occupies more liminal spaces than most. While searching for a publisher, I was told more than once that it fell between two stools—into the liminal, if you will. It might be interesting and important, but it was not intended for a scholarly audience and was too challenging for a general one.

To the first part of this complaint I plead guilty. I take scholarship seriously, but I did not write this book as one scholar to another. There's nothing wrong with doing that, and from time to time I have done so myself. But scholars aren't the only ones interested in challenging ideas. Back in the eighteenth century, every educated person had some acquaintance with cutting-edge philosophy and science and tried to keep up with literature and art. I would like to think that such readers still exist, and I wrote this book for them: people who may have no professional background in religion, philosophy, or biology but who wonder about the nature of religion and spirituality and of the human species itself, people who are willing to look at their own assumptions and ideas and rethink them if needed. All that I ask of readers is an open and active mind.

The conventional wisdom, though, seems to be that the general reader wants entertainment, the occasional bit of new information, and the pleasant shock of an unexpected connection or two. They have minds that open just a little bit, and they enjoy a gentle stroll around the block, but they need to be protected against anything too strenuous or novel. They prefer books that leave things pretty much as they were before.

It would be a sad world if this were true—and a dangerous one. New, complicated, or challenging ideas should not be kept locked up in the academy like criminal lunatics. They need to be introduced to the public at large, made part of everyday conversation, and be tested in the thoughts and experiences of people with intelligence and curiosity but no special expertise. If we writers cannot help this happen, we're falling down on our job.

Judging from publishers' lists and the shelves of our shrinking book-stores, the general reader certainly shows an interest in science and religion, and these topics, religion especially, involve the deepest and most difficult of questions. Religion, after all, is a human attempt at coming to grips with what is truly real; and what could raise bigger and more challenging ideas than the nature of ultimate reality? Surely it is in this area that nonscholarly books should provoke rethinking and self-examination.

Sadly, though, there's little to challenge the reader in most books on science and religion. Their writers tend to belong to one of two camps; they are either imperialists or boundary commissioners. The imperialists want one practice to swallow up the other. One set of imperialists claims that religion is just an inept way of providing the knowledge that only science can reveal. For these new atheists—Richard Dawkins, Daniel Dennett, and Sam Harris come to mind—science should be our only method of inquiry, and religion needs to vanish.

The other set of imperialists insists that science is a doomed attempt at establishing the ultimate truths, which are found only in religion. They seem willing to write off science as little more than a species of engineering. In either case, the offending practice is simply explained away, demoted to a position of such unimportance that we need not feel threatened by any of its now-discredited insights.

The boundary commissioners, on the other hand, think of science and religion as two different ways of generating useful information that differ primarily in their subject matter. For them, the task of the science-religion debate is to draw appropriate lines so our scientific toes don't step on our religious ones and vice versa.

All these writers assume before they set out that science and religion have a lot in common. They can pit one against the other because they think of both of them as systems of explanation. This makes sense to them because they, like most of us, believe that people are independent, self-sufficient, rational beings who take in information, weigh the consequences of different courses of action in the light of their immediate and long-term goals, and act as they choose. All that we really need is good and accurate information, and that's what both science and religion claim to provide. The question that propels the science-religion debate is which of the two has the right to make that claim.

As this book tries to show, however, both contemporary biology and most if not all spiritual traditions agree that this picture is wrong and deeply misleading. It is all the more surprising, then, that few books on science and religion share that insight. Whatever challenges they make to our ordinary ideas, they never question our ordinary beliefs about the kinds of beings we are and the ways in which we make our way through the world. What's equally rare is any sense that there is something behind both science and religion that can't be approached through the pursuit of knowledge and that can't be turned into information—something irreducibly liminal. That's why the science-religion debate does not seem to get very far. It's based on a mistaken theory about human nature and the role of concrete knowledge, and it shies away from the in-between space where creativity, insight, and wisdom have their source.

The great philosopher Immanuel Kant said that his philosophy grew from three questions: "What can I know?" "What ought I do?" and "For what may I hope?" We usually think that religions are meant to answer those questions, and that assumption is all but universal in the science-religion debate. What I would suggest instead, though, is that religions do something totally different, something that may sound unscientific but that is absolutely necessary. They teach us to stop looking for answers altogether. Instead of solving questions, they show us how to live with them. They put us deeply into the problematic nature of life and keep us from stepping back out again like a timid swimmer at the beach. They place us in the wordless in-between until we can no longer settle for partial or misleading solutions.

The aim is not to leave us in perpetual suspense, like the ancient Skeptics who withheld judgment on everything. It is, instead, to unravel our grasping for answers until experience itself makes them unnecessary. As the philosopher Ludwig Wittgenstein—himself deeply concerned with questions of religion—once wrote,

> The solution of the problem of life is seen in the vanishing of the problem. (Is not this the reason why those who have found after a long period of doubt that the sense of life became clear to them have then been unable to say what constituted that sense?)[1]

This has happened to innumerable people throughout history, but it requires a long and patient residence in the in-between.

There is a gap between what we are and know and what we can think and say. This is one of the darkest and most productive of in-between spaces, and language itself would not exist without it. As China Miéville's *Embassytown* brilliantly suggests, our inability to say the truth is what makes language a vehicle for creativity and an instrument of freedom, and this is a lesson that goes beyond the philosophy of language. Our conscious life can never fully or accurately grasp reality. That is a good thing; its richness depend on that very failure.

That is the liminal space where religious practice takes us. It is a hard place to live in—for most of us an impossible one—but it is not so hard to embrace the ideas that such a realm exists and that it is good and useful to lay thought aside, open ourselves to it, and learn from it. Yet it can be difficult to explain this to people in the West, even sincerely religious people, because among us everything seems to turn into words.

This is due in large part to the long and fundamental influence that Christianity has had in Europe and in the places that Europeans have colonized, settled, or influenced. Christianity relies on language and doctrine in a way that few other spiritual traditions do. Even more than the other monotheistic religions, Christians expect people to guide themselves by their ideas about things. As a result, the task of religion appears to be to teach the correct, absolutely true ideas that will guide people in proper ways. Words have to communicate the truth. If they didn't, they would not be able to lead us to salvation.

We in the West get many of our most cherished and least examined notions of who and what we are from Christianity. Thanks to its long cultural influence, even the most antireligious of westerners are likely to make the same assumptions about human nature and the role of language and thinking that Christians do. This is clearly what's going on with those atheist writers who have dominated the science-religion debate. Although they pose in all sincerity as proponents of impartial, universal reason, their ideas of human nature and the mind are eerily similar to those of Christian theologians. In exactly the same way, their ideas about religion are as provincial and Eurocentric as the most culturally insensitive missionary's. The religion they attack turns out to be little more than Christianity—and a very narrow form of that tradition at that. They have no feel for the life of other traditions or for much of the life of Christianity itself.

This causes problems for our thinking about religion. If we're going to understand humanity's spiritual life in all its chaotic variety, we need to confront those problems squarely. We in the West need to step away from the ideas and assumptions that we, like the atheists, have picked up from our Christian heritage. We need to move ourselves into a liminal zone where we can get some perspective on both Christianity and the religious realms outside it. And that, too, is where this book hopes to lead the reader.

Within that zone, all kinds of distinctions fade into insignificance. I will not be talking about textual religions versus indigenous religions or about great traditions and those of the masses. Far more than on doctrine and idea, I want to concentrate on the nature of religious experience itself, whether it is the experience of the teller and hearer of myths, of the Buddhist monk, of the dervish, of the hunter on a vision quest, or of the Indian housewife lovingly offering scent, light, flowers, and fruit to her chosen deity. Such experiences are more than emotional states. They have their own logic and their own form, and they show us things about how these people feel and make their worlds. By opening up a wider range of human experience, they can show us something about the nature of reality itself.

I have tried to chart a relatively straightforward path through all these liminal spaces, but the nine chapters that follow fall into three groups of three chapters each. The first three are concerned with clearing the air. They examine some of the new atheists' claims, critique their biological and philosophical presuppositions, and show how these tie into the specific assumptions and habits of thought that we've inherited from Christianity. The "scientific" view of humanity that all the critics of religion share is that we're information-processing, thinking agents. They may cast doubt on our belief that we do all this thinking consciously, but their debunking leads to something very similar: the notion that we're independent, self-acting, information-processing systems who simply aren't aware of most of our thoughts. If we're not ideal agents, we're "lumbering robots" controlled by genetic programs, and these programs are the real agents. They're the ones who are processing the information and issuing the orders.

This is all but certainly wrong, for reasons that we'll examine in the first three chapters. But the new atheists' errors are common ones, and we need to build a different foundation from the ground up before we can understand human nature and religious practice in any other light. The next three chapters do that work. They suggest a new starting point for talking about what we really are, bringing out the inherent intentionality and knowingness of all life and the limitations and built-in errors of self-consciousness.

The last three chapters show how spiritual traditions evoke this inherent knowledge and awaken us to the life of the body, examining their unique approaches to language and the transformative work of embodied spiritual practice. At the end the argument comes full circle, offering some thoughts on the kinds of ethics and politics that might emerge from the vision outlined here.

To reach that point, much must be surrendered. Spiritual experience can be seriously unsettling. It drives us to set aside our deepest ideas about who and what we are and what kind of knowledge we can aspire to. Everything must go. Then we can see what is left, what reality might feel like if we stopped trying to capture it in thought. At the center of the book, then, in the middle of Chapter 5, is a reversal. This is the heart of my argument: that we are not individual agents who base our actions on our symbols and images of a world outside of us but aspects of an impossibly vast collaborative, collective activity that both acts and comes to self-knowledge in the body. We are not apart from the activity of the whole of things, and our deepest nature is one of identity with everything else. This is hardly how we see ourselves, but the opening towards this vision has been a characteristic of religious life from the earliest practices we know of, and it is also consistent with much modern biology.

To understand this changes our picture of religion, too. The world's religions do not offer revealed knowledge or communion with a world of disembodied spirit. They are made up of concrete practices that orient us to the wisdom of the flesh, the embodied knowledge that escapes reason and evades every form of conscious thinking but that silently guides and shapes our lives. They are meant to make us live differently. Doctrines are always secondary, always meant to be laid aside in the end.

This is a lot for a small book, and I thank those who have helped me in the writing. Nothing I write or do could be done without the love and support of my wife, Loret Gnivecki Steinberg, and if it could be, it would nonetheless lack much of its savor and delight. It was a special gift, too, to send the chapters on biology to my father, Bernard Steinberg, for his review. In his professional life my father was a microbiologist, and that is one reason—though not the only one—that this book is dedicated to him and to my mother Ruth.

Our daughter Sarah Falkner, a writer herself, was as always a keen supporter and a keener critic. Michael Francis Gibson, another writer and a fellow traveler along some of the same roads, sought me out in time to offer both needed criticism and most welcome enthusiasm. Others also read and commented on earlier drafts, and my thanks go to Martin Barr, Karen Findling, Franlee Frank, Janet Ginsburg, Brian Schuth, and Andrew Nash—though I know that Andrew is not so comfortable with how it all turned out.

But this book is also a record of my own intellectual and spiritual exploration. Those who have studied the subject will recognize the influence of German idealist philosophy on my thought, especially that of Johann Gottlieb Fichte. Dan Breazeale, Tom Rockmore, and all the other members of the North American Fichte Society have been tolerant of my historian's bent, accepted me as a fellow scholar, and shown me innumerable ways of thinking and rethinking that most extraordinary thinker of a most extraordinary period. I also want to thank Celia Applegate of the University of Rochester's

Department of History and the hardy handful of students who weathered my course on "German idealism in historical context."

Writing this book led me to a deeper engagement with the practice of yoga and meditation, too, and I owe much to everyone at the Kripalu Center for Yoga and Health. A special mention should go to Stephen Cope, who welcomed the ideas that found their way into much of this text. My most intense and fruitful experience there, though, was with the therapist and meditation teacher Judith Blackstone. She also read an earlier version of the book, and I am thankful for her support, but those thanks are as nothing compared to the debt I owe to her for her teaching. Judith's psychological insights and her deceptively simple and subtle meditation techniques continue to open doors for me; her Realization Process, as she calls it, is one of the most efficient and powerful paths to the real that I have ever encountered.

As the writing drew to a close, though, I found that I needed something more. The ideas in the book made sense to me, but I knew that they needed to be practiced with others. They needed to be danced and sung, not just thought about. For a few painful minutes, I imagined that I would have to go on pilgrimage somewhere, travel to India or some such place, and find out what it actually felt like to live as if these ideas were both true and of central importance. Yet within a day of that disconcerting discovery, I found what I could never have imagined was possible: a South Indian temple based on ideas remarkably like those outlined here that was both traditional and radically egalitarian, with a welcoming community of devotees who were eager to teach, and that was only a twenty-minute drive from our home in upstate New York.[2]

For the past few years, then, I have had the extraordinary privilege of spending most Saturdays in a world that, though it is not India, is more Indian and Sri Lankan Tamil than it is anything else. The first draft of this book was completed there, and its final shape owes much to my experience of temple ritual and of regular practice in the South

Indian tantric tradition of Sri Vidya, so similar in its underlying philosophy to the vision of the German idealists. I am deeply grateful to everyone there and to my guru Caitanyananda—Aiya or "Mr." to all of us—I owe a debt that I can never repay. It is through Aiya's guidance that I have come to taste what little I have of the reality of things and the unity that is not apart from its infinite diversity, the reality that every tradition draws closer to in separate ways but that we in the temple approach through the auspicious figure of Sri Rajarajeshwari, the esteemed monarch of monarchs. I do not expect any of my readers to follow me to her, but for me, at least, she is the starting point to which the book leads. My hope is that it will lead others to starting points that are equally fertile.

Notes

1. Ludwig Wittgenstein, *Tractatus logico-philosophicus*, trans. D. F. Pears and B. F. McGuinness (London: Routledge, 1961), 73, sec. 6.521.
2. The temple is lovingly described and analyzed in Corrine G. Dempsey, *The goddess lives in upstate New York: Breaking convention and making home at a North American Hindu temple* (Oxford: Oxford University Press, 2006).

1

Should We Abolish Religion?

In early 2009, the world's first "atheist bus" made its debut on the streets of London, England. An ordinary double-decker in the city's bus fleet, what made it newsworthy was the slogan it carried: "There's probably no God. Now stop worrying and enjoy your life."

Comedy writer Ariane Sherin and biologist, author, and critic of religion Richard Dawkins, who came up with the slogan,[1] must have thought that they were striking a witty blow at religious belief, but in reality it was nothing but a mobile testament to their ignorance and provincialism. God as a big bully and a cowering faithful who are terrified that one false move will land them in hell make up nothing more than a very unconvincing caricature. Sherin's and Dawkins's pointed jab missed its target completely.

Considering that Dawkins is one of the most prominent of the so-called new atheists, along with Sam Harris, the philosopher Daniel Dennett, and the late journalist Christopher Hitchens, and considering how often he writes and speaks on the nature of religion, he might have been expected to show a little more insight into the things that draw people to religious in the first place. How could he be unaware that many religions don't have a hell to worry about? How could he not know that believers often speak of prayer and ritual as joys so great that earthly pleasure palls? Why didn't it occur to him that the elimination of the divine from their lives would leave many people bereft instead of relieved?

The truth of religious claims is one thing, and we'll be discussing that throughout this book. But what religious experiences have meant to people is another, and here, at least, it's obvious that Dawkins and his associates are talking through their hats. To many people the atheist bus slogan must have sounded something like, "You can't get nourishing and tasty food anywhere. Now stop worrying and go eat at McDonald's."

From the evidence of this much-ballyhooed campaign, Dawkins and his associates simply don't know what religion is about. Their ludicrously narrow picture of a fundamental human activity is one thing that makes it so depressing to plod through Dawkins's *The God Delusion* or the texts of the other "new atheists." As we'll see later on, what is even more damaging is that most of what passes for science in their books isn't good science, either.

It's not that many apologists for religion are much better. Their idea of religion is too often drawn from Christianity, and this keeps them from grasping the very different forms of religious life and practice in the non-Christian world; they write as if every question comes down in the end to a factual one, whether or not God exists. Their treatment of science is equally blinkered. Because of Christianity's strong emphasis on a deity who brings the universe into being out of nothingness, they tend to cherry-pick bits of physics and cosmology to "prove" his existence by the details that science can't explain, an exercise that ultimately proves nothing. On both sides, then, the science-religion debate is more heat than light. Science is bigger and more problematic than many scientists think, and religion is broader and less dogmatic than many believers believe.

Religion certainly demands some kind of explanation, though. We don't know of any community that doesn't do *something* that can be called religious, although very few of them set it off in a special corner the way we do. But what accounts for this universality? The religious often tell us that everyone has a religion because God is real and is active everywhere, but this kind of begs the question, and it fails to explain why He or She is seen and experienced so differently in different places. From the secular, scientific perspective, we're often told that life has almost always been mysterious, painful, and terrifying, and religion gives us at least the illusion of comfort and security in a dangerous world. It's just primitive science, fated to pass away with the triumph of rationality.[2] Dennett, more philosophically astute, theorizes that we're hardwired to assume that there's an agent behind everything. This helps us prepare for possible attacks from predators or enemies, but it also leads us to think that storms, volcanic eruptions, and the bright blue sky must be produced by some intelligent entity or entities.[3]

Mistaken theories or relief from fear, though, don't explain the bliss of the religious experience. This, too, has been a human universal—or something close to it. Devotees in innumerable cultures insist that their practice grants them moments in which they feel themselves to be unbounded, free, and spontaneously responsive to everything else, part of a different and better world where they are intimately known and loved. The world of that experience feels far more real than our own; everyday life looks like a shoddy fabrication. Only joy, love, and grace are true.

Is this a pleasant self-induced delusion or a glimpse of something genuine? The new atheists have their answer ready, of course, which is that it's all baloney. Yet they can't attack the experience itself—the bliss is genuine enough. Instead, they mark it down to oxygen deprivation or some other physiological state and move on to their real interest: the explanations that religious people give for those experiences.

The critics of religion usually start their attack here, telling us that there's no evidence for the factual claims that religious people make. It's a good place for them to start because on this count they're absolutely right. There isn't the slightest shred of scientific proof for the existence of heaven or hell or for the management of this world by an all-wise, all-knowing, all-powerful, and loving deity. The "proofs" of the existence of God you can read in philosophy texts are less than flimsy, as Dawkins is right to point out.[4]

But being right on this point doesn't do much for the atheists. If we're interested in experiences instead of explanations, the proofs of God's existence are beside the point. And many if not most religions make that choice. Those in indigenous communities are focused on changing the ways we see and feel, not with generating theories about the world. The same can be said about most Indian practices, where ideas are thought of as useful but treacherous stepping-stones.

There are exceptions, though, and the most important of these is Christianity. Christianity is preeminently the religion of explanation and discourse, the one most obsessed with pinning down the supposed facts of the divine. This doesn't make it better or worse than other religions, but it does make it a very misleading starting point or template for thinking about religious experience and religious life in general.

One of the problems with the new atheists is that they all do that anyway. Their assumptions and theories are no less Christian for being scrubbed clean of overt religiosity. They're more post-Christian than they are truly godless, and like the most insensitive kind of missionary, they see all religious life through the lens of Christianity.

Dawkins demolishes Christian theological claims with energy, skill, and persuasive humor, for example, but he's ill at ease with anything else. He doesn't say very much about Judaism or very much about Islam aside from frequent references to the Taliban and Osama bin Laden. He advises readers interested in "primitive" religion—the phrase is telling in itself—to consult the antiquated and wildly unreliable *The Golden Bough*,[5] and when he gets to Buddhism and Confucianism, which are not theistic and avoid truth claims, he suggests that they aren't really religions at all.[6] Dennett has similar problems, starting off *Breaking the Spell* with a definition that leaves out early Buddhism entirely and probably excludes Confucianism and Chuangtzu's Taoism, too.[7] And neither wastes any time on classical polytheism or Hinduism.

They are missing something important and revealing. Taoism, Hinduism, Buddhism, Confucianism, indigenous religions, and classical polytheism all have at least one thing in common. None of them tries to come up with hard-and-fast explanations about spiritual experience or ultimate reality. Polytheism is a way of approaching something too protean to be pinned down by the limited medium of words. Unlike the god of the monotheistic faiths, the gods of polytheism are not the final truth. They're images that help devotees grasp something truthful but unrepresentable concerning a world about which no final truth can be told. There's nothing inherently ludicrous in it and nothing implausible in the idea of a reality that we can experience but can't see, grasp, or describe. Polytheism is a very reasonable middle way between ignoring that "something" and embalming it in words.

And this brings up another important point. We have to be careful not to mix up the truth of an explanation with the reality of whatever it is that people are trying to explain. Just because we misinterpret something doesn't mean that the thing doesn't exist. There is no man in the moon, but the light and dark patches that make up his face are definitely real. Believers can't prove that the universe is under the charge of Yahweh, Lord God of Hosts, but that alone isn't enough to conclude that their experience of Him isn't a valid experience of something else.

This is a distinction that the critics of religion all ignore. They argue that because all factual statements deriving from religious experience are false—that is, because these don't give us accurate information about the "real world"—it follows that religious experience is a delusion. But this logic isn't valid unless experiences stand or fall with our explanations. This does *not* follow; in fact, it's an absurdity.

Dawkins and Dennett, though, really seem to think that words and experiences are the same thing. That's why they don't realize that disproving the factual claims of one or another religion says nothing about the significance of religious practice. Nor does it occur to them that religion might be a human universal because it's a rationally valid undertaking that happens to bring us into a condition that we can't adequately explain but that is nonetheless rooted in reality.

In other words, the failures of religious discourse don't invalidate religious practice. Everything positive that religious people say might be literally false—let us grant that they really *are* all literally false. It makes no difference. Religions may still be intelligent and efficient techniques for turning us toward an indescribable reality. This possibility isn't excluded by disproving any or all religions doctrines, and it is certainly unscientific to reject it before you set out.

It must be admitted that religious institutions are as much to blame as anyone else for this confusion between explanation and experience. There's a Zen Buddhist commonplace that you shouldn't mistake the pointing finger for the moon it's pointing to. The history of the "great" religions shows all too well why this warning is needed. Time and again someone will open a window on the deeper currents of reality. Within a few generations her insights become assertions, and she gets venerated as a god. In a few more generations a similar honor is bestowed on those who were especially fervent in their veneration. Texts and commentaries accumulate, and the study of words about other people's words about the experience replaces the experience itself.

Something of this sort is probably inevitable and even necessary; there's no other way to build a tradition, and traditions are useful things even if you want to do nothing but revolt against one. It is still a weakening of the original opening, though, and this kind of process has always been far too useful to those who are interested in social control. A canon and hierarchy serve the chief goals of any institution, religious or secular: self-preservation and growth. It is no criticism of religion, though, to say with Christopher Hitchens that it is man-made. Of course it is. *Every* system of explanation is man-made. Nobody else is in that business besides us humans.

The issue is different. It is whether the human practices that we call religious have anything to do with anything real. On this question the jury is still out. None of the false or unprovable things that religious people say about their experiences and no tendency toward institutionalized deadness can invalidate the experiences themselves. What we would like to know is what we can learn from these experiences when they're teased apart from our interpretations. We need to look past the gods, past God himself, and learn what, if anything, is there.

The falsity of religious claims is not the weightiest charge brought by Dawkins, Hitchens, and Harris, however. They argue that religion is not merely an error; it is a Bad Thing, and we need to do away with it. In his preface to *The God Delusion*, Dawkins writes with admiration of an ad that ran in connection with his television series *Root of All Evil*. It read, "Imagine a world without religion," and it showed the New York skyline with the twin towers of the World Trade Center still standing.[8]

This is the Bad Thing argument in a nutshell, and these days it certainly seems plausible. People do terrible things in the name of religion. Millions and millions of people have been killed in the name of religion, and every week thousands of stupid, nasty, dangerous, hateful, and ridiculous things are said in the name of religion by Christians, Jews, Muslims, Hindus, and members of other spiritual traditions. But was John Lennon right that things would be different in a world without religion—that we would live happily together and beat our swords into plowshares? Would tensions between nationalities and groups be easier to resolve and would people leave off massacring one another in the streets?

Dawkins's own example ought to make us think twice. The hijackers of 9/11 were Muslims, and they were likely to have espoused the Wahabist strain of Islam that we associate with Osama bin Laden. If you take the trouble to read what bin Laden wrote, though, you'd find that his reasons for attacking the United States had very little to do with religion and a lot more to do with international politics.[9] And if Dawkins were to respond that the chief sore point with bin Laden was the Jewish state of Israel and U.S. support for that state, I could point out that the inspiration for Zionism was not religious Judaism but nineteenth-century nationalism.

Zionism, in fact, was meant to take the religion *out* of Judaism. Its creator, Theodore Herzl, thought that the Jews had used religion to preserve their national identity and that once they were planted again in their own land this unnatural protective religious shell would dissolve and the Jews would become just another nation like the French or the Italians. Herzl was so irreligious that he didn't even have his sons circumcised. So the idea that Zionism is an example of religion at work has it backward.

This error is typical. Dawkins simply doesn't recognize how political most supposedly "religious" conflicts are. Neither do most of his allies. Here is a list that Sam Harris included in his "Atheist Manifesto" drawn up at the request of the Web site *Truthdig*:

> Palestine (Jews versus Muslims), the Balkans (Orthodox Serbians versus Catholic Croatians; Orthodox Serbians versus Bosnian and Albanian Muslims), Northern Ireland (Protestants versus Catholics), Kashmir (Muslims versus Hindus), Sudan (Muslims versus Christians and animists), Nigeria (Muslims versus Christians), Ethiopia and Eritrea (Muslims versus Christians), Sri Lanka (Sinhalese Buddhists versus Tamil Hindus), Indonesia (Muslims versus Timorese Christians), Iran and Iraq (Shiite versus Sunni Muslims), and the Caucasus (Orthodox Russians versus Chechen Muslims; Muslim Azerbaijanis versus Catholic and Orthodox Armenians).[10]

This is quite an indictment, but most of Harris's cases are not religious problems at all. They are postcolonial conflicts where religion has become a weapon in a political struggle.

Should you want some details, here is a partial and highly synoptic list.[11] We have already mentioned Palestine. The Troubles in Northern Ireland make no sense unless you remember that the Protestants there are mostly descendants of British colonists and that most of the Catholics descend from the indigenous population. Northern and southern Sudan are divided by religion as well as by many other factors, but the oil in South Sudan is even more significant, and the Darfur conflict saw pastoralist Muslims fighting Muslim farmers. Nigeria's conflicts are shaped by the location of its rich oil fields. Ethiopia and Eritrea were divided by the infrastructure and institutions set up by Italian colonial authorities in what is now Eritrea, and Ethiopia's interest is largely access to the sea; there's no significant religious issue, as both have roughly similar religious makeups. The Caucasus was a region of independent and culturally alien states that Russia conquered and colonized in the nineteenth century to keep British interests at bay. They have never accepted their incorporation into Russia, and the allegiance of the Russians who were settled there in the Soviet era compounds the problem. The terrible war in Chechnya was a failed war of independence that took on a religious cast as it ground on.

Kashmir is more complex, but today's split between Indian Hindus and Muslims really began with the 1857 Indian Mutiny and the retaliatory massacres of the Muslim ruling class by the British. In Sri Lanka, too, religious overtones entered into what was basically an ethnic conflict fed by Sinhalese resentment at colonial preferences for the minority Tamils.

The Middle East, like India, had its own more tolerant precolonial past; in the 1940s, 30 percent of the population of Baghdad was Jewish, and few Muslims cared about the differences between Shi'a and Sunni. And Iran is a classic case of neocolonial manipulation fostering the rise of political Islam. The United States brought about the overthrow of a secular populist government in 1953 and helped the shah in his ruthless suppression of anything resembling a secular opposition. It is true that after the Islamic Revolution of 1979, the Iranian communists were slaughtered, but the Ayatollah Khomeni was only finishing a job that the United States and the shah had begun.

Harris, Hitchens, and Dawkins are wrong, too, in charging that religions have made such conflicts worse, turning ordinary battles into massacres. The historical evidence supports a much more troubling explanation for these horrors. The problem isn't religion; it's civilization itself—the world made by farming.

For most of our past we humans were hunters and gatherers, and our communities were probably a lot like today's hunting societies— leaderless, consensus-based groups where women and men lived and worked more or less as equals. A few hours of hunting and foraging each day would yield enough for a plentiful and varied diet,[12] and warfare, though frequent, was limited in scope unless grudges get really severe. It was not an easy life or a safe one, but it was much better than what followed.[13]

The rise of agriculture and urban life brought with it kingdoms, armies, and priests. For the first time in history we find large-scale inequality. People who had once been independent hunters were now slaves or tenant farmers.[14] Their diets grew monotonous and unhealthy, epidemics ravaged the close-packed villages and cities, and women were confined to their homes and were expected to bear children in large numbers to supply cheap agricultural labor. (Among hunting societies too many mouths were a burden.) Social tensions must have been overwhelming and had nowhere to go. Hunting was reserved for the ruling class, who have kept it as their special privilege ever since. This was an explosive system, and it erupted periodically into a new kind of large-scale warfare, made more deadly by advanced technology and social regimentation, in which orgiastic slaughter was the reward of victory. The oldest evidence of large-scale killing is a mass grave at Jebel Sahaba in what is now the Sudan.

It is approximately 13,000 years old—about the time that agriculture began.[15]

This set a pattern for the future. The classical Mediterranean world was a paragon of religious toleration, but nonreligious massacres were accepted as normal. Odysseus, for example, took pride in the title "Sacker of Cities." He and his crews specialized in finding unprepared communities, overwhelming their defenses, and killing all the men and raping all the women. They would sell the children and the surviving women into slavery and keep the looted bronze, gold, jewels, and weapons for themselves. This is what made them rich and respected.

Odysseus didn't slaughter and rape for religious reasons. Neither did the Athenians in the Peloponnesian War; they sacked Melos for reasons of state. Hundreds of years later, Julius Caesar killed a million Gauls so that he could add their land to the Roman Empire, but he had no argument with their gods.

While the "Babylonian Captivity" is sometimes seen as a religious war, we can see from the book of Ezekiel that most Hebrew exiles in Babylonia were too comfortable in exile to consider leaving. We don't find specifically religious wars until Christians took over the Roman Empire. But even with sorry events like the Crusades and the persecution of the Cathars, it's hard to tell how much religion was the motive for killing and how much it was cynically used as a cover for more worldly interests.[16]

There has been plenty of nonreligious genocide in recent history, too, from Hitler and Stalin to Pol Pot and the Khmer Rouge, the slaughter of Tutsi in Rwanda, and many more. Civilization doesn't tame savagery; far from it. It brought us from a world of occasional individual cruelties to one of mass killing. When large armies are needed, it helps to have an ideology to rally the troops, and religion can serve this function very well. If it's not available, though, there are others that will do the trick—racism, an imagined or real history of oppression, imagined or real opposition to the glorious course of the revolution, or public health.

That religious institutions and their leaders have allied themselves with tyrants and have even launched their own wars of aggression weakens the case for the defense, of course, but it doesn't prove that religion *caused* these wars any more than there's proof that science caused the atom bomb, global warming, the pollution of the oceans, and many other disasters. On this count, the prosecution case must be rejected as not proven.

The critics have another charge, though. Even if it's not actively evil, they claim, religious belief keeps us from recognizing and dealing with the problems of the real world. Its promises of "pie in the sky" turn believers into sheep who passively accept their lot instead of changing it. It is the opium of the people, as Marx said.

Still, it is easy to mock wish fulfillment when your own life is comfortable enough to make other consolations available, like good food, good wine, or a house in the country. Is it fair to tell the less fortunate to lighten up and relax? When simply getting through the day is an act of heroism, a pinch of religious opium may have its place. Marx himself was of this opinion; what he actually wrote was, "Religion is the sigh of the oppressed creature, the heart of a heartless world, and the soul of soulless conditions. It is the opium of the people."[17] To ask for the abolition of religion, he argued, was to demand a world in which people would not need its consolations.

But religious life and expression are far more varied than this would suggest. Where religious expression most earns our respect is precisely when it rejects false hope or the insistence that everything will be fixed and forgotten in heaven, the way Job rejects his comforters in the Hebrew Bible. Religion can demand of us that we confront reality in all its messiness and its brutality, and it demands of reality that it show itself to us in all its terrifying purity. It grasps the ungraspable contrarities of human life, its simultaneous perfection and brokenness. It does not turn us away from life; as Jesus promised, it give us one that is more abundant, more real in all its terrors as well as all its joys.

In funerals, where we want acknowledgment of our sorrow even more than a promise of future happiness, religions retain their monopoly. For all the power of the state and all the emotional commitment that individual citizens made to the Soviet project, the Soviet Union's attempts to craft a Communist funeral were failures.[18] An example from *The God Delusion* may suggest a reason. Surprisingly, Dawkins closes his preface to the paperback edition by describing the Order of Service (his capitalization) for the funeral of a 17-year-old fan:

> A lone piper played the Manx lament "Ellen Vallin." Two friends spoke eulogies. Dr. Ashton himself [the boy's father] recited Dylan Thomas's beautiful poem "Fern Hill" ("Now as I was young and easy, under the apple boughs"—so achingly evocative of lost youth). And then, I catch my breath to report, he read the opening lines of my own *Unweaving the Rainbow*, lines that I have long earmarked for my own funeral.[19]

It sounds very dignified, thoughtful, and quite in the tradition of the Church of England. It may well have been as moving as funerals get in a social sphere where anything louder than a stifled sob is considered an unseemly show of emotion.

But how can such a ritual help us live with something as unacceptable as the death of a beloved son? It is our emotional demand for the impossible that funeral rituals evoke, accept, and resolve. To live fully, we need to tolerate and ultimately accept the intolerable and the unacceptable. There can be no catharsis, though, unless we open ourselves to the depths of our sorrow and loss, and so far we have found how to do this only in religious ritual. Contrast the secular funeral above with a funeral in a church of fervent believers, such as an African Methodist congregation, and what bursts forth in song and preaching in the latter is neither wish fulfillment nor servility but the full pain and grandeur of being human.

Of course these emotions are irrational, and of course what is intolerable and unacceptable is only our refusal to accept the world as it is. The rational response is that of the Roman general who, on being informed of the death of his wife, said only, "I knew when I married her that she was mortal." Death is inevitable, pain is most often random, and suffering is most often pointless. Shouldn't we realize that it is childish to want our husband or infant with us once more and that life and death are unfair only because we want life on our own terms?

That most rational of religions, Buddhism, would seem to agree; it enjoins a total detachment in which only a compassionate pity for others' useless suffering remains. But this can be as inhuman as any other scientific rationalism or dogmatic religion that would deny us the right to grieve. As R. H. Blyth, the wonderful English writer on Zen, complains, all we are left with is " 'Thy will be done' in infinitely meaningless inanity":[20]

> I remember being told of a man dying of leprosy, whose face was all eaten away, but who continued to repeat liplessly and almost audibly, "God is love! God is love!" This, if a true story, is a remarkable tribute to the value-creating power of human beings, even greater than that of Christ on the cross, but one would hardly dare to go around to a leper hospital saying such a thing to the people there.[21]

Like Job, who would neither praise God nor curse him, we want the world to make sense, and we expect justice to prevail no matter how often we are reminded that the opposite is just as likely, if not more so. We cannot help but judge the world by inappropriate standards. Who would live in a world where we did not?

To be human is to be haunted by a perfection in which we are truly at home but that we know we cannot inhabit. There was neither an Adam nor an Eve, but we are all fallen just the same. And there remains a garden in Eden, too. Religious practices open us to the felt knowledge of that perfect unity, plenitude, and bliss without denying the equal reality of cruelty, starvation, and pain. Through them, we can feel the world as just and unjust and, as Nietzsche said, equally justified as both. That is where Job found his peace: in clarity of vision rather than in explanations or comforting thoughts.

No reasoned or sensible philosophy can accommodate both the effortless rightness of things and their fearful injustice. We are deeply united, but we are just as deeply solitary. The world is perfect as it is, but its pain is incessant and unbearable. It seems to many that our world is the shadow of another world of fullness, stillness, and joy, without loss or injustice. We are exiled from that world, but some religions teach that we are destined to return there, and others try to bring us to see that we have been there all along.

But already we're getting into explanations. What counts is that duplicity, the mysterious presence of that other world that illuminates but does not cancel out our own. The sense of another world can be a psychological crutch, of course, but it is also and always a structural necessity. The logical framework and the vocabulary we need to face our predicament come from religious experience, and out of those resources we have made art, poetry, and drama that speak past the culture-bound images of any particular cult.

The reality of the other world can call this world to judgment, as it does in the prophetic traditions. It may leave nothing appealing or worthwhile in the world at all; one thinks of the god-intoxicated *sadhus* of India, meditating in caves or wandering naked, indifferent to life's pains and pleasures. But the other world can be just as powerful in its absence. The nineteenth-century English Jesuit Gerard Manley Hopkins wrung some of his greatest poetry out of those depths:

> No worst, there is none. Pitched past pitch of grief,
> More pangs will, schooled at forepangs, wilder wring.
> Comforter, where, where is your comforting?
> Mary, mother of us, where is your relief?
> My cries heave, herds-long; huddle in a main, a chief
> Woe, world-sorrow; on an age-old anvil wince and sing—
> Then lull, then leave off. Fury had shrieked "No ling-
> ering! Let me be fell: force I must be brief."

> O the mind, mind has mountains; cliffs of fall
> Frightful, sheer, no-man-fathomed. Hold them cheap
> May who ne'er hung there. Nor does long our small
> Durance deal with that steep or deep. Here! creep,
> Wretch, under a comfort serves in a whirlwind: all
> Life death does end and each day dies with sleep.[22]

But the perfection and the rightness of the other world is hard to bear, too, because it seems to care nothing for our own wants and desires. The stories of Genesis tell of the necessary but disturbing unfairness of things, the theme magnificently developed much later in the book of Job. The patriarch Abraham reproached God himself; "Shall not the judge of all the earth do right?" he demanded.[23] The Lord accepted Abraham's advice on that occasion, but His own sense of right rarely corresponds to ours. His favorite Jacob took ruthless advantage of a father's blindness and his older brother Esau's simplicity, stealing first the birthright and then the all-important paternal blessing. Jacob is the hero of the story, but our hearts go out instead to the guileless, victimized Esau:

> And he said [to his father], Hast thou not reserved a blessing for me? And Isaac answered and said unto Esau, Behold, I have made him thy lord, and all his brethren have I given to him for servants; and with corn and wine have I sustained him: and what shall I do now unto thee, my son? And Esau said unto his father, Hast thou but one blessing, my father? bless me, even me also, O my father. And Esau lifted up his voice, and wept.[24]

Although the Talmudic rabbis detested Esau and never missed a chance to concoct terrible stories about him, the writers of Genesis were clearly more sympathetic. He deserved better, but the future lay with Jacob instead, and the future, as always, was pitiless.

Esau got off lightly compared with Ajax in Sophocles' play of the same name. Before its action starts, Athena has cast him into a murderous but shameful insanity to protect her darling Odysseus. Ajax, the hero of the Trojan War, now slaughters cows and tortures sheep, thinking that they are an army massed against him. When the goddess exhibits him, Odysseus is moved to pity at the suffering of his sworn enemy: "I see the true state of all us that live," he tells her. "We are dim shapes, no more, and weightless shadows."

Athena is not so moved. She leaves the stage with a steely warning:

> Look well at this, and speak no towering word
> Yourself against the gods, nor walk too grandly . . .
> One short day
> Inclines the balance of all human things
> To sink or rise again. . . .[25]

Ajax, too, does not deserve his fate. His grandeur, like that of Antigone, Oedipus, or Heracles in the horrifying *Women of Trachis*, is that he comes to accept that fate and make it his own. At the close of *Oedipus at Colonnus*, the blinded Oedipus walks unaided into blazing light. In such a moment, the absolute rightness and bliss of the other world and its terrifying impersonal force are one and the same. Oedipus is already a god.

Without the other world, though, without the gods and inescapable destiny, there would be no tragedy in these plays and no mystery in Genesis. These stories would become dramatized Lemony Snicket instead—a Series of Unfortunate Events. We know that things could have been otherwise, but without the gods ruling over us we could not say that they *should* have been otherwise. Nor would tragic heroes accomplish anything by rising above their own selves and willing what the gods have willed. Sophocles' plays would be reduced to acknowledgments that shit happens.

Among hunting people, where life is by and large easier and social relations are more pleasant, the gap between human and divine is not so wide or deep. The play of the two worlds is often intimate, even sexual, and the distance between them inspires sadness rather than tragedy. For the Haida of the North Pacific coast of North America, the

spirit world of the animal-people is much like our own. The two worlds
are bound together with love and longing, but they are also always pulling apart. Myth tales relate the entanglement of the two and their endless dance of consummation, separation, and loss, as in the story by the
poet Ghandl that Robert Bringhurst translated as "In his father's village, someone was just about to go out hunting birds." It is a Haida
variant of the widespread story of the Swan Maiden, the same folktale
that lies behind Tchaikovsky's ballet.

A hunter falls in love with a goose-woman and she with him, but
she leaves him when her father's gifts of food in time of famine are
belittled as "goose food":

> She went where her skin was.
> Then she flew.
> She flew in circles over the town,
> and leaving her husband sickened her heart, they say.
>
> And then she passed through the sky.
> After that, her husband was constantly weeping, they say.
>
> An old man had a house there at the edge of the village.
> He went there and asked,
> "Don't you know the trail that leads to my wife?"
>
> "Headman's son, you married a woman
> whose mother and father are not of this world."[26]

Though he passes through many tests and wins his wife back, the
hunter cannot stay in her village either. The two love each other,
and they deserve happiness. But at the end of the story they are
apart, as they must be. She is alone and he is a seagull on a shoal,
cut off from everything he loved and squawking incessantly.

What all these poets knew and what Dawkins, Dennett, Hitchens,
and Harris fail to see is that religion is just as much a critique of the
world as it is a submission to the divine. This is a virtue that outweighs
many faults. Fatuous and dangerous pronouncements and sexual and

gender-based repressiveness have been based on bad science as often as on bad religion; the rhetoric of racism and racial separation was founded on crackpot anthropology, eugenics, and studies of brain size much more than on a few biblical texts about the children of Noah. But the virtues of religious metaphors have not been duplicated. As yet, there is nothing else that lets us think through the human predicament. There are times when we need to live outside the preconceptions and delusional goals of our little, self-created selves. There are times when we need to call the judge of all the earth to account, and nobody else will do. At the very least, then, religions appear to rest on deep psychological truth.

Providing insight into the human mind and heart or imagery for even the deepest art would not satisfy the partisans of religious belief, of course. They want us to recognize that religions are true but also that they are Good Things. For advocates like President Eisenhower, all religions are good indiscriminately; he asserted in 1954, "Our government makes no sense unless it is founded on a deeply felt religious faith—and I don't care what it is."[27] Others pick favorites, like the writers of the Yale Korean course I once attempted. "Yes, Buddhism is a fine religion," went one of the sentences I failed to memorize, "but Christianity is the true religion."

But what is Good about religious experience? Aside from comfort and aside from the depth of experience it embraces, we are told that it calls us to compassion and to serve others and that it grounds us in an ethical life that would otherwise find too little nourishment.

This would be worthwhile if it were true, and there is arguably a religious inspiration to many social movements. Socially conscious Britons like Mill, Martineau, and Darwin and the American Jews who passionately supported the civil rights movement were each only one generation removed from a deeply religious milieu.

On the other hand, most religions have had little trouble accommodating themselves to the ethical norms of the time. Paul wrote, "There is neither Jew nor Greek, there is neither bond nor free, there is neither male nor female: for ye are all one in Christ Jesus"[28]—yet 1,600 years later, every Christian church still tolerated slavery. Even the Society of Friends took a century to decide that it was a sin. Muslims and Confucians were long content with locking women up, and Hinduism is deeply implicated in India's caste system.

Most of the time, religion figures look like followers in ethics, not leaders. Ethics generally aren't taught anyway; each community seems to have its generalized, unspoken consensus about what you should do and what you should avoid, which is what makes social life tolerable. For complex reasons, this cloud of ethical norms changes through time, and sometimes religious leaders are the first to pick up the new norms and sometimes they are the last.

But what right do they have to lead anyway? Unless spiritual leaders work by example, the way Gandhi did, their claims to authority on ethics or any other subject have to rest on access to truth. So we're back to the question we asked at the beginning of the chapter: Are religions about something real? Or are they nothing more than oddities of a system that evolved to do something else, malfunctions of body chemistry, or psychologically necessary whistling in the dark? We already know what Dawkins and Dennett think. But before we accept their answers we might want to take a closer look at their own credentials.

Notes

1. The organizers' own website has all this information: http://www.atheistbus.org.uk.
2. This very nineteenth-century view is shared by Sam Harris.
3. Daniel C. Dennett, *Breaking the spell: Religion as a natural phenomenon* (New York: Penguin, 2007), 109–12.
4. Richard Dawkins, *The God delusion* (New York: Houghton Mifflin Harcourt, 2008), 100–36.
5. Dawkins, *The God delusion*, 57, 219.
6. Dawkins, *The God delusion*, 59.
7. Dennett, *Breaking the spell*, 9.

8. Dawkins, *The God delusion*, 23.

9. See, generally, Bruce Lawrence, ed., *Messages to the world: The statements of Osama Bin Laden* (London: Verso, 2005).

10. http://www.truthdig.com/dig/item/200512_an_atheist_manifesto.

11. The literature on each of these conflicts is voluminous, and I hope the reader will forgive the absence of references here.

12. Marshall Sahlins, *Stone age economics* (London: Aldine-Atherton, 1972), chap. 5.

13. Stephen Pinker's *The better angels of our nature: why violence has declined* (New York: Viking, 2011) appeared too late for me to consider it, but it appears to concern itself almost entirely with events after the development of hierarchical societies and agriculture.

14. The most celebrated essay on this subject is Jared Diamond, "The worst mistake in the history of the human race," *Discover*, May 1987, 64–66.

15. Douglas P. Fry, *Beyond war: The human potential for peace* (Oxford: Oxford University Press, 2007), 53; F. Wendorf, "Site 117: A Nubian final Paleolithic graveyard near Jebel Sahaba, Sudan," in *The prehistory of Nubia*, ed. F. Wendorf (Dallas: Southern Methodist University, 1968), 954–87.

16. The Fourth Crusade, for example, was a commercial war between Venice and its rival Constantinople.

17. Karl Marx, "A contribution to the critique of Hegel's philosophy of right: Introduction," in *Karl Marx: Early writings*, ed. Quintin Hoare (New York: Vintage, 1975), 243.

18. Catherine Merridale, *Night of stone: Death and memory in twentieth-century Russia* (New York: Viking Penguin, 2000). See also Paul Froese, *The plot to kill God: Findings from the Soviet experiment in secularization* (Berkeley: University of California Press, 2008).

19. Dawkins, *The God delusion*, 21–22.

20. R. H. Blyth, *Zen and Zen classics*, vol. 1, *From the Upanishads to Huineng* (Tokyo: Hokuseido Press, 1960), 123.

21. Blyth, *Zen and Zen classics*, 14.

22. Gerard Manley Hopkins, *Poems, now first published*, ed. Robert Bridges (London: Humphrey Milford, 1918), 63.

23. Genesis 18:25; all quotations are from the Authorized King James Version.

24. Genesis 27:36–38.

25. Sophocles, *Ajax*, in *The complete Greek tragedies: Sophocles II*, trans. John Moore (Chicago: University of Chicago Press, 1957): 13, ll. 125–32 (reprinted with permission).

26. Ghandl of the Qayahl Llaanas, *Nine visits to the mythworld*, trans. Robert Bringhurst (Vancouver: Douglas & McIntyre, 2000): 87, ll. 104–14. From the poem "In his fathers village someone was just about to go out hunting birds" from the book *Nine visits to mythworld: Ghandl of the Oayahl Llans*, volume 2 of the *Masterworks of the classical Haida mythtellers trilogy*, © 2000 by Robert Bringhurst, published by Douglas & McIntyre: an imprint of D&M Publishers Inc. Reprinted with permission from the publisher.

27. Cited in Will Herberg, *Protestant-Catholic-Jew* (Garden City, NY: Doubleday, 1955), 97.

28. Galatians 3:28.

2

Those Who Come to Mock

Neither Dawkins nor Dennett realizes that ignoring religious practice leaves a hole in their critique. This is a very revealing blindness because it is connected with a master metaphor that both of them take all too literally: they see people as biological computers. They think that all sentient activity, human and nonhuman, is the manipulation of symbols and information. Decision making, daydreaming, theory concoction, conversation, hunting, play, art appreciation, sexual activity and fantasy, cooking, meditating, and everything else that we and other animals do in a directed, intentional way—all of it can be reduced to information processing.

This isn't a neutral or unproblematic image. It implies specific theories about life and reality, and relying on it has some serious consequences. It starts with a decisive separation between inner and outer worlds and assumes that everything that happens in the outer world is meaningful to us only after it's turned into symbols or other representations in the inner one. This cuts out anything that words or images can't express or identify and puts the words or images in the place of the experience itself. Next, it is almost always presented along with the assumption that life can be understood as the activity of a control system—a root program or process that runs everything. The control system is the executive at the heart of the inner world. It takes information in from the outside, analyzes it, and tells the body what to do.

These assumptions are so common today that you may take them for granted. If that's the case, I hope you'll set them aside until you've read a little further; you may find that they look less obvious and less attractive the more you think about them. This is especially important because they're some of the key assumptions that most religious practice tries to dispel.

To explore how this picture of reality works and how its affects the case against religion, we'll focus on Richard Dawkins, whose biology and theory of "memes" lie behind several critiques, Daniel Dennett's included. A geneticist and a prolific and popular author, his ideas first reached the general public in 1976, when he published a book titled *The Selfish Gene*.[1]

This title was meant to be shocking, and so is the book. *The Selfish Gene* flings an in-your-face challenge to our sense of self-importance. We think of ourselves as gifted and special beings who can be anything we choose to be and who can rise above our biological needs and chart our own course through life. Nonsense, says Dawkins. We're just another temporary product of natural selection, and natural selection cares nothing about us. In fact, it cares nothing about any organism. All it "sees" are "replicators"—molecules that have "learned" to reproduce themselves. The ones that you and I harbor are genes. They run *everything*. We, by contrast, are barely more than puppets.

At its heart, Dawkins's theory is like the old joke about a chicken's being the egg's way of making more eggs. Since genes get passed down from generation to generation, they're immortal. Evolution is about *them*, not about the perishable organisms that house them. Successful genes propagate and spread through the population, and failures disappear. All that organisms like us are good for is passing genes from one generation to the next.

A body, wrote Dawkins, is merely the clumsy machine that genes build to reproduce themselves:

> Now [replicators] swarm in huge colonies, safe inside gigantic lumbering robots, sealed off from the outside world, communicating with it by tortuous indirect routes, manipulating it by remote control. They are in you and in me; they created us, body and mind; and their preservation is the ultimate rationale for our existence. They have come a long way, those replicators. Now they go by the name of genes, and we are their survival machines.[2]

We happen to be lumbering *self-conscious* robots, but aside from our self-consciousness and size, we're no different from a cockroach, a toadstool, or a paramecium. When our genes say jump, we jump.

You might think that Dawkins has run straight into the chicken-and-egg conundrum. He wouldn't agree. Since he assumes that life is about information, he has to conclude that the data coded into the genes produce the organisms, not the other way around. By Dawkins's definition, then, life began when genes built their first primitive "survival machines," when ancient self-replicating molecules coalesced into groups and learned to grow bodies.

Other people have looked at the same facts and drawn different conclusions. We know that long ago the oceans of the primordial Earth teemed with tiny, self-organizing microspheres and other stable structures, chemical bubbles that spontaneously emerged and maintained themselves. These looked something like cells, but nobody would call them alive; their self-organization simply happened because of the shapes and properties of the molecules that made them up.

Some of these bubbles eventually began incorporating short chains of RNA, a molecule that can act as a template for making proteins. Thanks to the proteins cooked up from the RNA's recipes, these microspheres kept their structure intact for longer times and through a wider variety of conditions than those who did not have RNA in their interiors. Scientists call these "protobionts," the first steps towards life. But each of these was a special creation, with neither parents nor children, so they can't really be said to have been alive.

RNA molecules have another property, though: they replicate themselves. The basics of life—self-organization, the maintenance of identity in changing environments, and reproduction—came together when the first mother protobiont split into daughter protobionts with identical structures, contents, and RNA. Later protobionts made use of DNA, another molecule with its own set of protein recipes, instead of RNA, and this is when biological history itself is said to begin. But the three elements of RNA protobiology still define life in the world of DNA.[3]

It's the combination that counts. We can't really say that either the self-organizing microspheres or the self-replicating RNA came first. (It's worth noting that the RNA did not dictate the structure of the protobiont.) As the biologist Denis Noble argues, it's simply arbitrary to claim that life began when replicators invented survival machines. It would be just as true to say that living organisms captured colonies of genes because they wanted their protein recipes.[4] Life began with the synergistic union of these two different elements. Neither can be ignored, and the organism can't be reduced to one or the other.

There's no logical or scientific reason to reject the insight that life began with a combination of organism and genes. But Dawkins does. He writes organisms out of the story from the very start, seeing evolution in terms of information systems that get more and more complex and fine-tuned through natural selection. Genes come first because their DNA contains data. Microspheres do not.

This heavy emphasis on information marks *The Selfish Gene* as a product of its times. It was written at the very beginning of the computer age, and it's soaked through and through with computer metaphors, the new language of information processing, and the market ideology that began to emerge as the postwar industrial boom faded. Genes are master programmers, Dawkins writes, and they're programming for their lives. They have designed an uncountable number of different robot models that compete against one another for survival. Natural selection weeds out the failures. Successful genetic programs, then, design robots that produce more new robots than other program do, which of course means that there will be more of the winning gene's duplicates in the next group of robots than its competitors manage to put in place.

But the genes don't build their survival machines and then wait around for the next generation. They not only design the robots; they program the robots' behavior as well. This is Dawkins's real innovation. Most of his other ideas are not far from the mainstream of biology. He writes, for example,

> "Good" genes are blindly selected as those that survive in the gene pool. This is not a theory; it is not even an observed fact; it is a tautology. The interesting question is what makes a gene good. As a first approximation I said that what makes a gene good is the ability to build efficient survival machines—bodies.[5]

Language aside, this is uncontroversial. A finch whose beak is well suited for cracking seeds will outperform and outreproduce another seed-eating finch with a less efficient beak, and in time there will be more and more finches with the better beak. Dawkins is merely giving a gene's-eye picture of this example.

He is claiming something more, though. In his view, a gene doesn't have to spread through the population because it leads to a useful adaptation. In fact, the gene doesn't really have to produce any physical change in the organism at all. A selfish gene can triumph simply by programming a strategy for its robot that gets a lot of selfish-gene copies into the next generation's gene pool. Like those modern celebrities who are famous for being famous, the selfish gene is successful because it succeeds.

The most obvious way the gene can do this is to ensure that its robot manufactures lots of little robots, which means fighting off attackers, eliminating rivals, and having lots of sex. Dawkins's genes would rather be carried by men because in a given amount of time a male can pass a lot more genes down to the next generation than a female can. It is obvious that this theory provides a ready-made explanation—or rationalization—for human aggression and competitiveness. But Dawkins argues that there are more subtle ways of helping our genes along than living a long life and having a lot of kids. We can help and defend other family members.

Siblings share more of our genes than cousins do, and cousins share more of our genes than do nonfamily members. When you come to their aid you may think that you're honoring family ties or acting out of love or concern. It's pretty to think so, Dawkins might say, but you're falling prey again to the human illusion of self-importance. The real reason that you're your brother's keeper is that your brother has more of your own genes than anyone else. Being nice to him increases the odds that *some* of your genes will be well represented in the next generation. Once again, you're doing what your genes tell you to do, and you're serving their interests—not your own and not your kin's.[6]

This is no exaggeration. Dawkins writes, "If an individual could be sure that a particular person was his identical twin, he should be exactly as concerned for his twin's welfare as for his own." And the intricacies of calculating one's degree of genetic kinship with others don't faze him, although he cautions, "What really happens is that the gene pool becomes filled with genes that influence bodies in such a way that they behave as if they made such calculations."[7]

Altruism, then, is really something purely selfish—only it's the genetic program that's acting, not ourselves individually. Tear off the mask of self-regard, and instead of free, rational creatures, we find ourselves to be tools of an impersonal information system that cares only for the statistical distribution of specific chains of DNA. Our own inner life is a lie. Personal ambitions, hopes, and dreams are just ways to increase our attractiveness as reproductive partners and thus to maximize our genetic posterity. Human institutions on every scale, from the family to the church all the way up to the nation-state, are simply ways of maintaining a separation between in-group and out-group so our precious gene pool doesn't get diluted. Even self-sacrifice is a strategy. It's either a way to pile up IOUs that can be cashed in later or a gamble that you'll get to pass more genes on to the next generation by passing up present advantages.

Many people have found this argument persuasive. It has a strong contemporary resonance and may feel almost self-evident since it draws on common images like the brain-as-computer and the competitive marketplace. But it is not correct and it simply *cannot be* correct.

Remember that we're no longer talking about a gene that codes for a beneficial trait. The selfish gene does nothing for the organism. All it does is increase its own chances of being present in the next generation. But a selfish gene that doesn't code for any other advantage is self-defeating. Dawkins's theory comes up against the fallacy of composition, which is the problem with standing up at a concert: if everyone else stays in their seats, you get a great view, but if a lot of people follow your example, nobody is any better off.

Success in Dawkins's terms means getting more of your genes into the next generation than your friends and neighbors do. But if you owe this success to the strategy coded by the selfish gene, your descendants will find themselves saddled with an ever less useful genetic strategy in an ever more competitive world. The "winning" selfish gene will end up in more people with each new generation. Eventually, so many people will be using its strategy that it stops conferring any advantage at all. It's undone by its own success.

This isn't to say that a selfish-gene strategy couldn't exist or maintain itself. In some circumstances, it may become common enough that walking away from the strategy would be difficult. Still, a more efficient or safer way of life will confer greater and more lasting advantages on a population than a mere talent for intraspecies competition. Finches with the better beak will produce more young than those with a less efficient model simply because they use less work to get the same nutrition and live longer, healthier lives. They use the environment better and thus live in a more abundant world. The selfish-gene scenario, by contrast, sees evolution as a zero-sum game, where my victory is your loss, and you can't have a zero-sum game in which everyone is a winner.

What's more, Dawkins is thinking entirely in terms of individuals within a given species. Evolution, though, is at least as concerned with different populations within a given environment. The most cunning strategy for one-upping your neighbors is all but meaningless when a competing species moves in. At that point the real issues are biological efficiency and a sustainable relationship with local resources, where social solidarity may do a species more good than a drive for competitive advantage.[8]

Another problem with Dawkins's theory is that we have no idea how genes could affect behavior in such detail. This is an especially big problem because he expects animals to recognize some pretty distant relatives. Proponents claim that there's statistical evidence consistent with the results of their model, so there must be *some* mechanism linking genes with behavior—we just haven't found it yet. There's no way to disprove this, but there are other explanations for our special interest in family and friends that don't require us to postulate kinship detectors and calculators programmed into our genes. Simply growing up and living close to others changes the way we feel about them. The incest taboo, for example, seems to depend on this instead of genetic closeness. Siblings who are separated at birth don't have the same sexual inhibitions as those who grew up in the same home, while children who have been raised communally are rarely attracted to their nurserymates—they all feel like brothers or sisters, even though they're not biologically related.[9]

Perhaps the biggest problem with the selfish-gene theory, though, is that natural selection doesn't see genes anyway. It sees traits. We're lifted up or weighed down in the race for survival by the shape and functioning of our body and the efficiency of our behavior. Dawkins's theories might be more plausible if genes correlated directly to these traits. They are not. The path from one to the other turns out to be unbelievably complicated and involves many more factors than his theory can cope with.

Dawkins's picture of genes as programmers and the rest of the organism as their creation is wildly oversimplified and ultimately misleading. Genes don't really do *anything*. They're recipes for making proteins, which are the chemicals we use to keep ourselves going, and like most recipes, they sit quietly in their biological file box until they're needed. And if the genes were anything like a program, their code would be hidden beyond the wildest dreams of IT security specialists. Genes are long chains of DNA, so long that if a single one were stretched out, it would stick out on either side of us for a foot or so. To fit within the cell nucleus, they're folded over and over until only certain portions are exposed. These are the only parts of the gene that are active. This means that the way the gene is folded is as important as its contents.

What's more, those exposed portions don't contain straightforward codes for specific proteins. They contain code *fragments* called exons, and the exons on a single gene can be combined to make many different proteins. Even a single gene, then, is actually more like a recipe book than a single recipe. And just as we make several different menus from our favorite recipe books, depending on what we feel like eating or what's in the market, so does the cell make different proteins from the same gene, depending on the age of the cell and the state of its environment, both internal and external.[10]

It's misleading, then, to think of genes as blueprints for cells, traits, or bodies. Instead, they're just one portion of a dynamic, complex system. Each cell has a surprisingly large number of diverse but interdependent constituents. It needs the genes in its nucleus, but to go on living and acting it needs a lot more besides, including its complexly structured cell wall, the contents of its cytoplasm, and specialized

organelles like the mitochondria. As geneticists Eva Jablonka and
Marion J. Lamb write,

> We now know that a whole battery of sophisticated mechanisms is
> needed to maintain the structure of DNA and the fidelity of its rep-
> lication. Stability lies in the system as a whole, not in the gene. More-
> over the gene cannot be seen as an autonomous unit—as a particular
> stretch of DNA which always produces the same effect. Whether or
> not a length of DNA produces anything, what it produces, and where
> and when it produces it may depend on other DNA sequences and
> the environment. The stretch of DNA that is "a gene" has meaning
> only within the system as a whole. And because the effect of a gene
> depends on its context, very often a change in a single gene does not
> have a consistent effect on the trait that it influences. In some individ-
> uals in some conditions its has a beneficial effect, in other circum-
> stances it is detrimental, and sometimes it has no effect at all.[11]

The cell also needs neighbors. Everything one cell does is influenced
by proteins and other chemicals that wash over it from the others
close by. And extraordinary new research is suggesting that epigenetic changes, where DNA expression is altered because of factors
like nutritional levels, temperature, and humidity, can actually be
passed down to future generations—overturning a long-held belief
that this was impossible.[12]

This is not the only part of the puzzle that Dawkins neglects. No
matter how different they look and how differently they function,
every cell in our body carries the same genes. Until recently, we had
no idea how the undifferentiated cells of the early embryo turned
into muscle, nerve, bone, skin, liver, kidneys, and all the other different tissues it takes to make up a complex organism. We do now,
thanks to a branch of biology generally called "evo-devo" (from *evolution* and *development* by way of a 1970s band). Evo-devo research has
shown that the developing embryo is shaped by overlapping protein
baths that start from different locations and spread in different ways.
The regular patterns produced by the interaction of these protein

baths lead to regular patterns of cell growth, differentiation, and movement. Many factors determine what an embryonic cell does, and the most important is where it starts out in the little ball that all but unerringly turns into a living being. Here, too, it's not the genetic blueprint but when and how the genes are switched on and off that determine the result.[13]

To understand genetics, then, we need to think in terms of interconnected systems that constantly define and redefine themselves. The genes and organelles in every cell are linked in feedback loops, cells interact with one another in the same way, and these connections tie every level of organization with every other level. There's no way to disentangle one part from another. It's the same with the body and its organs and systems, and similar feedback loops unite the organism with the environment. The skin is a permeable membrane, after all, and there's much more passing through our senses than information.

Throughout the life of an organism, causation runs both ways, seamlessly flowing from the gene to the environment and from the environment back down through the switches that turn genes on and off. This is a profoundly open view of life, and it's completely different from the picture that Dawkins paints. In his account we are all shut off from one another.

Let's return to his "lumbering robots" passage with a different emphasis:

> Now they swarm in huge colonies, safe inside gigantic lumbering robots, *sealed off from the outside world*, communicating with it by tortuous indirect routes, manipulating it by remote control.

When Dawkins is focusing on specifics he's usually open to a more subtle and multicausal analysis, but his large-scale statements continue this theme of control from within. He sees organisms as closed systems with a privileged, internal control module. Our behavior is supposed to be determined by the genetic program that made us, and we use its resources to cope with an alien world outside.

In the real and very messy world of nested levels and feedback loops, though, there's no real inside and outside, no control level, and no place for storing blueprints. We have to give up looking for the system that regulates everything else. Where, exactly, is the "information" for making a cell? Is it in the gene? Is it in the pattern of folding that exposes certain exons that code for specific proteins? Is it in the organelles that determine which proteins are made from those exons at specific times? How about the systems, some of them in other genes, that influence *those* parts or the cell's surroundings and the chemicals that flow in and out through the cell membrane? The answer, of course, is "all of the above." The information to make the cell is present in all parts of the cell. It isn't localized in any control system, genetic or otherwise. The cell *is* the information, and the information *is* the cell. As Noble says, "The Book of Life is life itself."[14]

This digression into biology is important for another reason. Once we understand the assumptions behind Dawkins's biology, we can better appreciate his ideas about—well, ideas. Let us return, one last time, to the lumbering robot passage, now with the emphasis on the last phrase:

> Now they swarm in huge colonies, safe inside gigantic lumbering robots, sealed off from the outside world, communicating with it by tortuous indirect routes, *manipulating it by remote control.*

As Dawkins explains it, genes can do their work only before their robots go into production, so they stock our robot brains with rules to cope with the things we're likely to encounter throughout our lives, rules like "stay away from bright hot things that give off a smoky smell" or, if you're a spider, "spin threads according to the following knitting pattern and wait until you feel vibration in some but not all of the threads."

In more advanced models like humans, the genes install a learning system, too:

> One way for genes to solve the problem of making predictions in rather unpredictable environments is to build in a capacity for

learning. Here the program may take the form of the following instructions to the survival machine: "Here is a list of things defined as rewarding: sweet taste in the mouth, orgasm, mild temperature, smiling child. And here is a list of nasty things: various sorts of pain, nausea, empty stomach, screaming child. If you should happen to do something that is followed by one of the nasty things, don't do it again, but on the other hand repeat anything that is followed by one of the nice things."[15]

The trump card in the gene game, though, was the invention of a brain that could generate and get infected by "memes."[16] This is the other novelty in *The Selfish Gene*, aside from the selfish gene itself.

A meme is supposed to be a unit of culture. It's anything that can be taken up by the mind and varied or repeated. Dawkins's initial list was "tunes, ideas, catch-phrases, clothes fashions, [and] ways of making pots or of building arches." As others have noticed, though, the pots and clothes drop out of the discussion pretty quickly. When people talk about memes today, they're almost always talking about ideas, self-sufficient packets of information that are supposed to shape our thoughts and conduct.

Dawkins likens these fragments or tags to the early genes in their primordial soup (microspheres have no role to play in his story, you will recall). Memes are self-replicating cultural units floating in the soup of human culture. There is evolutionary pressure on these units, just as there is on genes, and those that infect many minds will survive. Those that have less sticking power will die out.

In *The Selfish Gene*, Dawkins adopted a colleague's summary as his own:

Memes should be regarded as living structures, not just metaphorically but technically. When you plant a fertile meme in my mind you literally parasitize my brain, turning it into a vehicle for the meme's propagation in just the way that a virus may parasitize the genetic mechanism of a host cell. And this isn't just a way of talking—the meme for, say, "belief in life after death" is actually realized physically, millions of times over, as a structure in the nervous systems of individual men the world over.[17]

In Dawkins's view, we are doubly programmed. The structure and makeup of our bodies and the broad outlines of our behavior are programmed by genes, the old replicators, but our conduct is also programmed by the new replicators: memes, messing around in our brains like little mental bugs.

But what exactly is a meme? They're ideas, of course, but just as it's frustratingly hard to pin down the contents of any particular idea, it's hard to pin down a meme. Take "belief in life after death." Muslims and Christians generally think that life after death is a good thing, at least for the saved; they associate it with clouds, harps, and eternal bliss. Hindus and Buddhists are less keen on the idea. Life after death means reincarnation, and the cycle of death and rebirth is a constant round of suffering. This one meme has completely different meanings, depending on its cultural context.

So does the "God meme." It presumably refers to the deity of the three major monotheisms. But Muslims, Jews, and Christians say such different things about their Gods that it's hard to imagine them as one and the same. To cope with this variability, we might try to replace our meme with the submemes God_m, God_J, and God_C. But even that wouldn't be enough. Those ideas vary within a single tradition, too, and they change over time. Since 1950, for instance, there's been a steady shift in the object of American popular belief from a distant lawmaker God to one who shares human joys and sorrows.[18] Within the submeme God_C, we would need to distinguish between sub-sub-memes God_{C1950} and God_{C2011}. But people simultaneously hold inconsistent or unclear ideas about most things, too, so perhaps we should develop a mathematical notation to show the ratio between these two in any American Christian on any given day. And this endless task gets harder because most of the time people just talk about God, plain and simple. How can we know what sub-sub-meme they're infected with?

If we really wanted to know, we'd ask, of course. Whatever else memes are—assuming for the moment that they are anything at all—the examples that Dawkins relies on are couched in language. And as soon as we pay close attention to words, we find out that language is a much more complicated thing than proponents of "memetics" think it is. Not only does Dawkins have a simplistic notion of how genes work; he also takes the same simplistic approach to language.

To be fair to him, it's easy to overlook everything that goes into even the simplest verbal acts. A word like "cow," for example, seems to point effortlessly to a large cud-chewing, milk-producing animal with soft eyes and a limited vocabulary. Most of the time, we assume that a conversation is a two-way exchange of information; when I say "cow," I'm sending a cow idea to you. From this commonsense viewpoint, memes seem plausible. A word is just a package containing what it means, so a meme is the meaning—the information—that can be found in its words.

But words, like genes, are nowhere near that straightforward. They, too, live only through the company they keep. If our parents and friends didn't use the word "cow" in specific ways—pointing to a page in a board book of farm animals and saying, "The cow goes MOOOO"; asking us to go to the barn to milk the cow; seeing a herd from the car window and wondering when the cows are going to come home; unkindly referring to a less attractive child as a cow; drunkenly proposing at night that we go cow tipping; or eulogizing a cow as a model of devoted motherhood—we wouldn't know what "cow" meant. Context is everything. The word "love" means different things in the sentences "I love this salad dressing" and "I love you," and nobody needs to be told that I don't want to set up a home with the salad dressing and spend the rest of my life with it.

As the philosopher Ludwig Wittgenstein said, the way we use a word *is* its meaning. Words get remade and transformed every time they're used and understood. And the context that gives them meaning includes actions, feelings, sensations, and every other aspect of our conscious and unconscious life. Many times, we grasp the precise meaning of a word from nothing more than our physical surroundings and emotions. That's why a small child's first words point to the people and actions that are most important to her.

Language is also used internally, in thought, but this isn't a matter of leaving the mind open for ideas that might flit by and infect us. Thinking is an activity. We are all aware of streams of sensation, a tidal flow of wordless and bodily experience that encompasses emotional states and much more. Within those currents, a restlessness may emerge, a cloudy kind of feeling that we can resolve only by "putting it into words." As we try out various constellations of words— we don't always bother with sentences—we gather together a group of meanings and relationships that conjures up something like the experience we started with. That's when we "know what we think."

The structure of human languages gives us rich resources for this task. No matter how much you try, though, you can easily be misunderstood. You may be able to evoke an experience for yourself through certain words, but the same words may not do the same thing for someone else. If you want to clear up this confusion, you'll offer, reject, add, subtract, and recombine words, passing them back and forth much as you did when you first tried to put your thoughts into language. If that process flows freely between two people, they may discover, after a while, that they're dwelling on similar experiences. That's when people understand each other: when words work the same way for both of them.

Communication is coordination of experience. It's not the exchange of information, where one person is a sender and the other a receiver. It's an action through which we join others along the same path, a mutual improvisation through which we fashion a dance. The basic structure of that action is a feedback loop. I am responding to your response to me.

Language lives in the give-and-take of our conversations. It lives, too, in the silent changes we work on one another through touch and smell and sight. As our experience changes our words take on new meanings for us. Every person who has been lucky enough to fall passionately and happily in love remembers the day that the touch of a hand completely unsettled everything they meant by the word. Less dramatically, every moment changes our perspective on our past and our surroundings, subtly but surely, and without our notice, our words quietly take on new shades of meaning.

There's no room for memes here. No word or phrase contains information in itself. None has an inherent content that forces itself on its users. Words play slightly different roles for everyone who uses them. Just as in biology, the information is a property of the system, not of the units. There are appealing or catchy ideas, of course, but it's the state of the world or the terms of our culture that gives one idea more resonance and staying power than another. Natural selection has nothing to do with it.

Memetics not only relies on a mistaken view of language but it paints an unrealistic picture of how we learn and act. For Dawkins, rules for conduct float around in a soup of thoughts, something like the little programs that run in the background of a computer. Action is a matter of matching up a perceived set of facts with the proper rule. According to memeticist Susan Blakemore, as Dawkins describes her ideas in *The God Delusion*, our "world [is] full of brains (or other receptacles or conduits, such as computers or radio frequency bands) and memes jostling to occupy them."[19] But how do we figure out what's meaningful in the world, and how do we choose one rule from the others? These are problems that Dawkins can't resolve.

We could try to salvage the concept of memes by thinking of them as semi-independent intersections of memory and desire, knots of past pleasures and sorrows and present-day hopes and fears that come to life under certain conditions and lead us to act in certain ways. There is every reason to think that such networks really exist and that they help define our world and guide our actions. But while

we may explain these to ourselves and to others by referring to verbal
tags like memes, the networks themselves come first, and they're intimately bound up with our personal and cultural history and deeply
rooted in our bodies and the real world we inhabit. We don't "get
infected" by a passing meme. We grab on to those that bring our
own emotions into focus, but they remain purely secondary, a frost-
ing on the cake of embodied thought and action.

The picture of minds filled with jostling memes is unconvincing,
and it's almost as silly as the one mocked by biologist and philosopher Maxine Sheets-Johnstone: "nonhuman primates have brains
capable of cooperative hunting"—"as if when summoned by hunger,
it is primate brains that go out to do battle on the savannah."[20] Of
course they don't; primate *bodies* do. And bodies are not brains, and
brains are not receptacles. Brains are not minds, either, and we ourselves are not brains. We are animate bodies that understand, touch,
smell, embrace, comfort, annoy, nurse, poke, and occasionally attack
one another, and we use our whole bodies to do all those things.
The kind of thinking that Dawkins and Dennett focus on is only a
part of this embodied life, and it plays a much smaller part than they
think.

Darwin understood this. While writing *The Origin of Species* he
went through his notebooks from 1838, looking for passages that
he thought would be useful. One of these was "Experience shows
that the problem of the mind cannot be solved by attacking the cita-
del itself.—the mind is a function of body."[21] It is a caution that
Dawkins and Dennett did not take to heart. They have no role for
the body at all. For them, it's just a dumb tool.

So what does all this have to do with religion? The answer is simple. If we really are computer-like minds that depend on information
and rules of conduct, then the only thing we care about is data, facts
about the world that we can work into our calculations and rules to
govern our actions. Religion would indeed be just another source of
that data, a rival to psychology or sociology if not to physics. It would

have to pass muster like any other body of information, and Dawkins, Dennett, Harris, and Hitchens take great pleasure in showing us that it doesn't.

If we aren't what Dawkins and Dennett think we are, though, this line of attack isn't justified. If our thoughts and words and the whole world of information are just parts of a larger and more complex galaxy of interconnection and action, experience itself becomes something that we need to pay attention to. How much of our life passes beneath the radar of our thoughts? How reliable are our ideas and pictures of ourselves? What possibilities are there for deeper and more genuine insight? Can we live more abundant lives, lives closer to reality? These are important questions, and their answers can't come in the form of theories. They have to come through different ways of living and seeing. That's where religious practices come into play.

Ironically, though, some of Dawkins's and Dennett's biases echo the target of their critique. Although they laugh at the mind/body dualism of Descartes and Christian theology, their own accounts are shot through with a brain/body dualism that's just as crippling. Everything happens in the mind, which Dawkins and Dennett, good materialists, identify with the brain. But though it's made up of cells just like our bones, muscles, viscera, and skin, their brain doesn't muck around with anything as messy as biology. It's an organic computer, and as with real computers, it's the software that counts. Hardware is secondary. The important thing about their brain is that it's stocked with programs, which means that they're talking about immaterial thoughts after all and not real organisms.

Dennett's mind/brain doesn't float up to heaven when its body fails, but it's just as independent of the body as the Christian soul is supposed to be. More than that, it is self-evidently the real individual, just as our real identity in traditional Christianity lies in our soul. In other words, both sides ignore living bodies. For both, we are nothing but the sum total of our thoughts, the activity of the supposed control centers or layers that bend everything else to their will.

Perhaps it is going to far to think of demonic possession when Dennett writes about "memeplexes" that take over our behavior for their own benefit and harm us in the process.[22] Even without that addition, though, he and Dawkins look like they're still tied to the ideas and assumptions of a Christianity that they thought they'd left behind. The science-religion debate is carried out within the old theological world of souls trapped in troublesome if necessary bodies. That may be why none of the critics thinks much about other religions and why that doesn't bother them. In their blindness to different traditions, they sound like updated echoes of the Yale Korean text. "Yes, Buddhism is an *interesting* religion," they might be saying, "but Christianity is the *paradigmatic* religion."

Notes

1. Richard Dawkins, *The selfish gene* (Oxford: Oxford University Press, 1976).
2. Dawkins, *The selfish gene*, 21.
3. This is generally recognized, and similar accounts can be found in most biology textbooks; see, for example, Neil A. Campbell, *Biology: Concepts and connections* (San Francisco: Pearson/Benjamin Cummings, 2006), 321.
4. Denis Noble, *The music of life: Biology beyond the genome* (Oxford: Oxford University Press, 2006), 18–22; here, Noble considers the passage from Dawkins cited above.
5. Dawkins, *The selfish gene*, 92–93.
6. This is generally called "Hamilton's law" after its brilliant and tragic formulator William Hamilton.
7. Dawkins, *The selfish gene*, 105.
8. To go any further in this direction, though, would take us into controversial areas of evolutionary theory that are well beyond the scope of this book.
9. This is well documented in the case of second-generation children in Israeli kibbutzim; see Yonina Talmon, *Family and community in the kibbutz* (Cambridge, MA: Harvard University Press, 1972), 157.
10. Noble, *The music of life*, 8–9.

11. Eva Jablonka and Marion L. Lamb, *Evolution in four dimensions: Genetic, epigenetic, behavioral, and symbolic variation in the history of life* (Cambridge, MA: MIT Press, 2005), 7.

12. Andrew Angel, Jie Song, Caroline Dean, and Martin Howard, "A polycomb-based switch underlying quantitative epigenetic memory," *Nature* 476 (August 4, 2011): 105–8, doi:10.1038/nature10241. A simpler account of the work can be found in Biotechnology and Biological Sciences Research Council, "Epigenetic 'memory' key to nature versus nurture," July 25, 2011, http://www.bbsrc.ac.uk/news/research-technologies/2011/110725-pr-epigenetic-memory.aspx.

13. A good popular introduction to this field is Sean R. Carroll, *Endless forms most beautiful: The new science of evo-devo* (New York: Norton, 2005).

14. Noble, *The music of life*, 10.

15. Dawkins, *The selfish gene*, 60–61.

16. Dawkins invented the word meme, and he wants it to rhyme with "cream."

17. Dawkins, *The selfish gene*, 206–7.

18. See, for example, Robert Wuthnow, *After heaven: Spirituality in America since the 1950s* (Berkeley: University of California Press, 1998).

19. Richard Dawkins, *The God delusion* (New York: Houghton Mifflin Harcourt, 2008), 228.

20. Maxine Sheets-Johnstone, *The primacy of movement* (Amsterdam: John Benjamins Publishing, 1999), 406. (Note that a revised edition of this book is available, but I have not referred to it.)

21. Charles Darwin, N Notebook, in Hoard E. Gruber, *Darwin on man: A psychological study of scientific creativity, together with Darwin's early and unpublished notebooks* (New York: Dutton, 1974), 331.

22. Daniel C. Dennett, *Breaking the spell: Religion as a natural phenomenon* (New York: Penguin, 2007), 84–85.

3

Getting Past Post-Christianity

This brings up another important issue. If we want to understand something about religions in general—if we want to say things that are valid not just for our neighbors and relatives but for people whose lives are almost totally unlike our own—then we need to guard against the danger of thinking "Christianity" when we say "religion." This is not a small job. Christianity is so much a part of our institutions and culture that even atheists have trouble shaking off its influence.

Nobody is free of partiality, but Christianity is a particularly poor starting point for comparative study. It is pretty much in a category of its own. It stands out even among the three Western monotheisms and not always in the ways that Christians used to claim. For example, only Christianity teaches that Adam's sin in the Garden of Eden doomed all his descendants to hell; neither Islam nor Judaism takes the fall so seriously, and both insist that God is eager to extend mercy.

In this respect, Jesus's parable of the prodigal son seems more Jewish than Christian. The wayward child spends his inheritance on riotous living and "comes to himself" among pigs who eat better than he does. Full of self-loathing, he decides to return and desperately rehearses the speech that he hopes will win back a little of his father's kindness:

> I will arise and go to my father, and will say unto him, Father, I have sinned against heaven, and before thee, And am no more worthy to be called thy son: make me as one of thy hired servants.[1]

As soon as he turns toward home, though, his father runs out to meet him, forgetting all his dignity in his overwhelming joy:

> And he arose, and came to his father. But when he was yet a great way off, his father saw him, and had compassion, and ran, and fell on his neck, and kissed him. And the son said unto him, Father, I have sinned against heaven, and in thy sight, and am no more worthy to be called thy son. But the father said to his servants, Bring forth the best robe, and put it on him; and put a ring on his hand, and shoes on his feet: And bring hither the fatted calf, and kill it; and let us eat, and be merry: For this my son was dead, and is alive again; he was lost, and is found. And they began to be merry.[2]

The father doesn't answer his son's words of repentance. It is enough that his son has turned toward home—the Hebrew word for "repentance" also means "turning." Such, says Jesus, is the mercy of our Father in heaven.

Scarcely two decades after the crucifixion, though, we find Paul telling the young churches that we can do nothing by ourselves. We can't even take the prodigal son's one step; all our attempts at satisfying God's demands only increase his righteous anger. But something extraordinary had happened, Paul adds: God himself had intervened in history to open the gates of forgiveness. By suffering and dying on the cross, God as Jesus had taken on himself the burden of sin that had consumed humanity since Adam. Jesus's blood had wiped the slate clean but (and it's an important "but") only for those who recognized this fact.

Paul stakes everything on facts, on the fact of Jesus's life and—especially—his death and resurrection. Jesus's own words slip onto the background as Paul hammers away at the world-historical meaning of his victory over death. "If Christ be not risen," he wrote, "then is our preaching vain, and your faith is also vain."[3]

From Paul to the present, Christianity has been a religion of facts—of ideas about specific things that have happened in the real world. Judaism may seem similar, with its stories about the Exodus and the

Ten Commandments and the divine grant of a homeland. But these have very little to do with the basis of Jewish religious life. They are facts after the fact, as it were. In Christianity, on the other hand, the factuality of Jesus's life, death, and resurrection is utterly central.

Gods who intervened in human history were not a novelty, of course. Quite the opposite: gods have always been meddlers. But exactly what they did or would do was always mysterious. Most of the time they went incognito, and nobody guessed that they were present until after they had gone. Near the beginning of the *Odyssey*, for instance, Athena disguises herself as a sea captain to visit Odysseus's son Telemachus. Telemachus welcomes this old friend of his father's and suspects nothing; gods being gods, their disguise is always perfect, of course. It is only when Athena leaves that he realizes, with a shiver, that he has just met with a god.

Even when they come openly, the gods surpass comprehension. In the great Indian epic the *Mahabharata*, everyone knows that Krishna is a god—the supreme god, in fact—but nobody is ever sure what his purposes are. His mysterious goals and his troubling tactics, which are harshly questioned in the poem itself, have been debated ever since.

The Christian god's intervention was something different. It was singular, decisive, and precisely defined. God had become not just man but one, specific man whose life was a historical event. The Nicene Creed is not content with the assertion that Jesus was crucified. Christians are to believe specifically that he had been crucified *under Pontius Pilate*. The detail is essential because it anchors the story in our own ordinary time.

There were good reasons for this emphasis on facts. The reality of Jesus's life, death, and victory was essential to the process of conversion. In the ancient world, conversions to one or another cult were not unusual, but these generally hinged on intellectual choice or matters of taste. Christian conversion was different. Paul and his companions came up with more than a new religion. In a very real way, they created a *new kind of religion*, a new vehicle of self-transformation that differed from the old ones because it depended on people's emotional identification with the story of a real person.

What were people looking for in Christianity? Paul, at least, addressed himself to those who felt helpless to overcome their selfishness and craving, powerless to leave off wounding themselves and others—people like Paul himself before his conversion:

> I know that in me (that is, in my flesh,) dwelleth no good thing: for to will is present with me; but how to perform that which is good I find not. For the good that I would I do not: but the evil which I would not, that I do. Now if I do that I would not, it is no more I that do it, but sin that dwelleth in me.[4]

And those who turned to the new church were worried about much more than a lifetime of bad deeds, guilt, and regret. The Hebrew Bible had said little about life after death, but by Paul's time most Jews had come to believe in an eternal afterlife of bliss or torment, a belief that probably originated with Zoroastrianism. Christianity inherited these ideas and harped on the fear of damnation with a relentlessness that no other religious tradition has ever surpassed. We all suffer some unease about the way we lead our lives, but to Paul this unease was proof that we were slaves to sin and deserved to suffer endlessly in hell. Not only were we sure to mess up, but God had no choice except to punish us eternally for the sins that we could not keep ourselves from committing.

The good news of the Gospels (a word which means "good news") was that God had offered us an escape from his own cruel justice. The Christian could die to her sins and be reborn into blessedness, just as Jesus had died and come back to life:

> Know ye not, that so many of us as were baptized into Jesus Christ were baptized into his death? Therefore we are buried with him by baptism into death: that like as Christ was raised up from the dead by the glory of the Father, even so we also should walk in newness

of life. For if we have been planted together in the likeness of his death, we shall be also in the likeness of his resurrection: Knowing this, that our old man is crucified with him, that the body of sin might be destroyed, that henceforth we should not serve sin. For he that is dead is freed from sin.[5]

This was not a literal death, of course. The conversion crisis was an exercise in vicarious suffering. The believer was to meditate on Jesus's own sacrifice until she could suffer as he did. She was to enact those events *in her thoughts*.

Such meditations must have been especially vivid in antiquity, when everyone knew the sights, sounds, and smells of sacrifice from childhood—the cowed or more often terrified animal clamoring under the chanted prayers, the sudden killing blow, blood on the floor and walls, the dismembered corpse, and the smells of blood, smoke, and burning fat. For many people, this was religion itself. "The worshipper experiences the god most powerfully not just in pious conduct or in prayer, song, and dance, but in the deadly blow of the axe, the gush of blood and the burning of thigh-pieces," wrote the historian of Greek religion Walter Burkert.[6] If we hope to appreciate the intensity of the early Christians' identification with Jesus, we should imagine his death as if it were an actual ritual sacrifice, different from the temple sacrifices of both pagans and Jews only in the infinitely deeper horror, pity, and shared responsibility that it calls forth.

Paul's Christianity thus rested on an exceptionally intense act of imagination, namely, the believer's identification with Jesus and her participation in his suffering, death, and resurrection. She was to admit the depth of her captivity to sin and accept responsibility for all her misdeeds, which included the most awful of crimes: the killing of God himself. As she envisioned what God had suffered because of her sin, the dread of damnation made her terror all the more unbearable. As Jesus accepted punishment for the sins of the world, she was to accept punishment for her own.

In that abyss of complete hopelessness and guilt, as she offered up her sinful life as a sacrifice, the believer would discover that God's mercy and love were infinitely greater than even her boundless capacity for evil. She would be reborn into the new life of the spirit. She had only to acknowledge the gospel truth: that a real event of incomparable horror and its extraordinary reversal into inconceivable joy had taken place in a real location on a given date—once and for all:

> If thou shalt confess with thy mouth the Lord Jesus, and shalt believe in thine heart that God hath raised him from the dead, thou shalt be saved. For with the heart man believeth unto righteousness; and with the mouth confession is made unto salvation.[7]

Such a confession of belief was not all that a Christian needed to do, but one could not be a Christian without it.

This conviction provided the force that broke open the believers' old life, and they could hardly achieve such a catharsis if they thought of the crucifixion as a mere symbol. They would not long for redemption unless they believed in the inevitability of damnation, and they could not understand why Jesus's life and death were so central unless they accepted the sacred history in which all the children of Adam were under a curse. These claims were necessary articles of belief in the way that we speak of belief today—as confidence that certain things are factually true.

Paul was surely preoccupied with spiritual transformation. But his letters are only part of the Christian Scriptures. These begin with the four Gospels, which were written decades later, in darker times, and in communities much closer to Jerusalem and the Jewish tradition than the cities of Asia Minor where Paul traveled. Mark and the other evangelists composed their books after the disasters of 70 CE, when a Jewish revolt against Rome had ended with the destruction of the temple, and after Jesus's followers had been rejected by the Jewish mainstream. As New Testament scholar Burton Mack has argued, they reimagined the crucifixion as a very special kind of martyrdom—one with a twist. It was not the triumph over sin and death that Paul preached. It was an act of cultural betrayal on the part of the Jews that would soon be reversed in apocalyptic triumph for those who knew Jesus as the Son of God.[8]

The new religion of Christianity ultimately fused Paul's focus on individual rebirth with the Gospels' cosmic-historical drama, but both strands relied on the factual reality of Jesus's death and resurrection. This is why these events had to be firmly anchored in historical time and the Christian account of cosmos and history had to be taken for ordinary fact. Ever since this dual origin, Christianity has been concerned about the opinions that people hold about the factual state of the world. The way we talk about "belief" and "faith" comes out of this new and unusual form of religious orientation. We rarely notice that few other religions share it.

Every aspect of Christianity is shaped by this unique method. It transformed the liturgy and the nature of prayer itself. Developed out of Jewish models, the forms they took on were so different from the original that today's Jews might find it hard to say how they were related.

We're familiar enough with images of pious Jews praying at the western wall of the Temple in Jerusalem to know what traditional Jewish prayer looks like, but the appearance conveys very little of the worshippers' experience. Jews are commanded to pray three times a day. There's a lot of text to be got through in even the shorter services, and the worshipper sits and listens only when the Torah is read.

Prayer is led, if one can call it that, from a platform in the middle of the room. The prayer leader is in the heart of the congregation, and everyone faces the same direction. His function is limited. The liturgy is divided into paragraphs, and the leader sings aloud the first and the last line of each paragraph as he, like everyone else, reads everything else on his own.

This gives the entire service a slow and mesmerizing rhythm. The majority of the congregation comes together at the end of one paragraph and the beginning of the next, only to drift apart in between. Since everyone is speaking aloud, if quietly, standing in the congregation resembles standing in the sea and bobbing up and down with the waves. The sounds of others' prayers ebbs and swells. Familiar phrases echo, pull together for a phrase or two sung to a favorite melody, and then are lost again into a heterophonic muddle. Even without understanding the words, the music of prayer itself can be emotionally involving.

The act of praying is even more so, and part of its strength is that it evades language even though it is made of words. From the beginnings of the synagogue, Jews have prayed in a foreign tongue—Jesus spoke and taught in Aramaic, not Hebrew. Even many observant Jews are not so fluent in Hebrew that they can parse the prayers as they pray.

This might seem like a deficiency, but it is the kind of deficiency that allows for something better to emerge. One's own mumblings and the larger rhythms of the congregation induce something like a trance (the rhythmic swaying of worshippers aids this), and the flow of half-understood words in the sacred language acts something like a Hindu mantra. Out of the blur of Hebrew, certain key words will surface over and over—the attributes of the divine and the worshipper's longings and thanks, for example. Since Hebrew is a Semitic language in which a single three-consonant pattern is used for many connected terms, those key words are often similar in sound and inevitably suggest one another.

Jewish prayer thus becomes a kind of collective guided meditation. Everyday experience is laid aside for a space, lulled to sleep by the music of mingled voices. Thoughts come to the foreground and subside in favor of others but not before they suggest a cluster of ideas that present themselves for contemplation and blend into those that emerge in the next section of the text. Since the concepts are few and rich, the experience of Jewish prayer resembles looking through a kaleidoscope, where the same shapes combine into an infinite number of patterns. But it is far less detached than this metaphor suggests. It is more as if one were *dwelling* in a kaleidoscope, blissfully immersed in an endless present where the community is fully absorbed in its appreciation of an inexhaustible perfection.

Something similar can be said of private devotions like the Rosary, but there is little or no room for these in the public worship of the Christian churches. If a Jewish service resembles a noisy collective meditation, a Catholic Mass resembles a theatrical performance. After the fourth-century Council of Nicea, when the church started to grapple with its new role as the state church of the Roman Empire, the service no longer centered on the assembled congregation. Now parishioners came as expectant spectators of a sacred event. They were present to witness the miracle of transubstantiation though which bread and wine were transformed into the body and blood of God himself and to be united as a community through imaginative participation in the divine sacrifice that this recalls. The eucharist thus echoed the conversion experience but at a much lower level of emotional intensity.

The mass places the central Christian mystery of the incarnation and self-sacrifice of Jesus *before* the worshipper. In other words, it can exist separate and apart from the worshipper. The most important Jewish prayers require a *minyan*, ten worshippers, usually men, but transubstantiation would still take place even if there were no congregation in the church at all. (Private masses and those said by the priest for himself are not uncommon, in fact.)

In Catholic theology, transubstantiation is also a fact, and whether it takes place is a question of canon law. It happens only when a properly ordained priest says mass. An imposter can dress in ecclesiastical garb and perform the ritual perfectly with real faith—but nothing will happen. The churchgoers who are victimized by such a hoax have no way of knowing if their attendance at mass was effective or futile unless they check with the authorities. Their experience means nothing.

What's more, the experience of taking communion is *created* by doctrine. It's a matter of the interpretation one gives to an experience instead of the experience itself. Transubstantiation is supposed to turn the substance of the bread and wine into the substance of Jesus's body and blood, but it leaves all the "accidents" untouched. Among the accidents, theologians include *"proper sensibles*—the excitants of the individual senses, colour for sight, sound for hearing, etc."[9] In other words, everything that we could possibly experience about the bread and wine remains the same. Only the way we think about them is different.

Like conversion, the eucharist is an act of the imagination. It takes place in the mind instead of the body, and what happens to a communicant depends on her ideas. Viewed strictly as an experience, communion is nothing more than a highly unsatisfying snack. It achieves meaning only if one believes oneself to be participating in Jesus's sacrifice by consuming the flesh and blood that he freely gave on our behalf.

For this reason, the eucharist can never appear intellectually naked, as it were. That's also why the mass is theatrical. Not only does it focus on an event that takes place before the awed gaze of the worshipper; it also provides a frame to define this event, using text and action—liturgy and ritual—so that the worshipper will give it the correct interpretation. For this reason, the order of the mass resembles the sacrificial rites of the Temple more than the communal worship of the synagogue. It echoes the rituals of animal sacrifice without the actions themselves: the ceremonies of purification and declarations of fitness and purpose, the offering, the sacrificial breach in the world of normality, and the catharsis and fellowship that follow in the shared feast.

Some of this emphasis shifted in the Middle Ages, when almost everyone in Europe was Christian and knew nobody but other Christians. Medieval Christianity had much more of a bodily character than its modern successors. Training and purifying oneself and shaping one's experiences were more important than matters of doctrine—which virtually everybody took for granted anyway. Talal Asad, a brilliant scholar of the concepts of religion and secularism, has written,

> The body, taught over time to listen, to recite, to move, to be still, to be silent, engaged with the acoustics of words, with their sound, feel, and look. Practice at devotions deepened the inscription of sound, look, and feel in his sensorium. . . . The proper reading of the scriptures that enabled her to *hear* divinity speak depended on disciplining the senses.[10]

This is not all that different from the way in which meditation and mantra repetition work to transform the devotee in the Indian traditions. In today's Christianity, though, such bodily discipline has been neglected in favor of an inner mental attitude. Over time, as Asad says, the Bible lost the character of "the materiality of scriptural sounds and marks" and became "a *spiritual* poem whose effect was generated inside the believer independent of the senses."[11]

This reached a climax with the Protestant Reformation, which made doctrine into the key to religious life. What *really* happens in the eucharist became a hotly contested issue. Catholics, Lutherans, Calvinists, and Anabaptists all fought—sometimes literally—over the degree to which and the way in which Jesus was or was not present in the host and the chalice. It seems incomprehensible to us that people would have been willing to kill and die over the dogma of the Real Presence, but in sixteenth-century Europe this was not so strange. The doctrine had answered some crucial questions: When we gathered in his name, how does God grace us with his presence? Has he genuinely forgiven us, and is the door truly opened to eternal life? Where is that door, and how can we pass through it?

For more than 1,000 years these questions had been answered. Luther, Calvin, Zwingli, and the other reformers made them into questions again, and everything truly important was once more at stake. If the eucharist was nothing more than a commemoration, then the way to blessedness that you had followed for all your life was a dead end. You weren't *really* purified by communion. Denial of the Real Presence threatened to empty this life of meaning and doom you to torment in the next.

Removing the mystery of the eucharist left a void in the middle of Christianity, and to fill it a new form of Christian worship emerged. The Protestant service, often stripped bare of the art and music that had heightened the pathos of the mass, developed its own transformative drama. Now, though, it took place solely in the hearts and minds of the congregation. The climax of the Sunday service became the sermon.

The reformed churches spoke to the worshipper's individual experience of God's presence. The eucharist might be taken literally, or it might be demoted to a symbolic gesture in memory of Jesus. Regardless, the focus of attention was now the worshipper's self-scrutiny as she listened to the sermon and took it to heart.

Yet not much had really changed. The sermon led the congregation back to the same kind of conversion crisis that had brought people into the church in the first place.[12] Every Sunday, parishioners were reminded of the immensity of their sinfulness so that, humiliated and humbled before God, they would be ready once again to accept the enfolding love of the crucified and risen Jesus. And perhaps because there had been no animal sacrifice in Europe for more than 1,000 years, Protestant preaching took up the theme of damnation and made it more prominent than ever. Psychic terror had become a mainstay of Protestant preaching well before Jonathan Edwards delivered his famous sermon on "Sinners in the hands of an angry God." It continues to create converts today on televised church services and webcast revival meetings, and the misery of the damned is crudely and powerfully depicted in thousands of fundamentalist pamphlets and comics.

In a way, the Protestants had only exchanged one form of ancient performance for another. Instead of the drama of sacrifice, the reformed churches embraced oratory, the art of rhetoric. As the orators of antiquity knew, people were rarely persuaded by rational argument alone. Artful presentation and a deliberate appeal to the audience's emotions were necessary. Marcus Antonius, grandfather of the Mark Anthony of Shakespeare's play, advised his listeners in Cicero's dialogue *De Oratore* that

> nothing is more important than to win for the orator the favor of the hearer, and to have the latter so affect as to be swayed by something resembling a mental impulse or emotion, rather than by judgment or deliberation. For men decide far more problems by hate, or love, or lust, or rage, or sorrow, or joy, or hope, or fear, or illusion, or some other inward emotion, than by reality.[13]

The same combination of rational argument and artful playing on the emotions is present in every good sermon and to the same end: to persuade the hearer of the truth of the speaker's cause.

Just like the sacrament of the eucharist, though, the life-changing sermon will leave you cold unless you accept the truth of its propositions. You need to believe in Hell before you can fear Hellfire, and you need to agree with the basic elements of Christianity to embrace the salvation that it offers to you. Adam's fall, sin, the necessity of blood, the incarnation, the atoning sacrifice, and Jesus's resurrection: these are all claims of fact, and to transform someone's life in anything other than a superficial way they generally need to be accepted as such.

For those who accept these claims, Christianity has tremendous emotional power. It presents us with a procession of images charged with so much feeling that they explode into art and music if we so much as think about them. Here are Adam and Eve fleeing the garden of Eden, the Virgin Mary with the divine infant at her breast, and Jesus's agonized, hopeless prayers in the garden of Gethsemane; Jesus arrested, crowned with thorns, mocked and beaten, and nailed to the cross, crying, "My God! My God! Why hast Thou forsaken me?" before he dies; the women at the empty tomb, unable to believe the angel who tells them, "He is not here; he is risen"; and the supper at Emmaus, when the disciples do not recognize their fellow traveler until he breaks bread and then vanishes—like Telemachus, they understand the visitation only in retrospect—and they ask one another, "Did not our hearts burn within us, while he talked with us by the way?"

Even unbelievers may find themselves moved to tears by these images. But religion is more than aesthetics. We can be equally moved by Andersen's "The Nightingale," when death gives the Emperor back his life so that he can hear just a little more of the bird's wonderful song, but we do not form churches to worship birds or Danish writers. Christian stories are meant to be true. They fill the world and the Christian's life with drama and color, but only as long as they are taken for history and not fairy tales.

Christians cannot escape this reliance on facts, even though that reliance opens them cruelly to the kind of criticism that Dawkins, Dennett, Hitchens, and Harris delight in. But these critics fail to see that while they reject Christianity as a religion, they accept the specifically Christian vision of humanity: that people are essentially fact-driven, isolated minds that crave and need accurate data and proper theories about the world. They also share a uniquely Christian idea of what religious life is all about. They think of all religions as more or less close approximations of Christianity—that they are all heavily tied to fact, for one thing, and are structured around the logical consequences of their doctrines. The problem with "religion," they often argue, is that it teaches us falsehoods about the world. It's got its facts wrong, and what we need above all are the correct ones.

Both our critics and many well-meaning students of "world religions" therefore assume that the first thing to know about any religion is what its practitioners believe. That is, they want a list of the propositions about the nature of the world and of people that are generally accepted as true by adherents of this particular "belief system." And this is a mistake. It forces all other traditions into the mold of Christianity. There is no easier way to misunderstand other religions and religious activity in general.

Although some adherents of religions other than Christianity could come up with a list of beliefs if forced to, many more would find the demand to be completely beside the point. Assertions of fact are simply not that important to them. Most non-Christian traditions can't be reduced to creeds or theories at all, and many of their sages go further and argue that creeds and theories are the height of *irreligion*. We shouldn't base our lives on *any* propositions about the nature of the world or of people. Belief systems are the problem, not the solution, and their religious practices are meant to break our habit of substituting beliefs and ideas of any kind for experience plain and simple.

Such a distaste for theorizing is common in Indian and East Asian thought. Western readers are most likely to have come across it in Zen Buddhism and its predecessors: the teachings of the great Indian Buddhist philosopher/monk Nagarjuna and the Ch'an schools in China. A seventh-century poem from China still commonly used in Zen centers and monasteries, the *Xinxinming*, states this theme as clearly as possible in its opening lines:

> The Supreme Way is difficult
> Only for those who pick and choose.
> Simply let go of love and hate;
> The Way will fully reveal itself.
>
> The Slightest distinction
> Results in a difference as great as
>   heaven and earth.
> For the Way to manifest,
> Hold not to likes and dislikes.[14]

The anonymous author makes no division between emotional preferences and theory, either.[15] We read, therefore,

> As soon as right and wrong arise,
> The mind is bewildered and lost.

R. H. Blyth's gloss on these passages may be helpful:

> There is no such thing as "the Truth." The nearest approach to any-
> thing like it is our state of mind when we desist from the search for it,
> and live our life. This is what the *Sutra of Perfect Enlightenment* means
> when it says:
>
> > Positive views are all perverted views;
> > All no-opinions are true opinions.
> >
> > And Yungchia says also explicitly,
> > Do not seek after the truth,
> > Do not cut off delusions.
>
> In every way the world is double, good and bad, profit and loss, here
> and there. But from another point of view, "There is nothing good or
> bad but our thinking makes it so." We are to stop this "thinking," this
> "having an opinion," this "judging." Yet if you say, this is the right
> view, this is the wrong, this the relative, this is the absolute, we are
> still "following" it. Truth is attained only when we realize that there
> is nothing to attain to. Eternity has its fulness of perfection in us only
> when we are engrossed in the temporal and imperfect.[16]

The *Xinxinming* is a guide to practice, a text to be used by meditators, and it warns practitioners about the danger of making even the
denial of truth into a truth and of straining after the enlightenment
that comes only when we stop seeking:

> Trying to still action
> Is an action itself.
> Still trapped in duality,
> How can you recognize oneness?
>
> ***
>
> No need to search for truth,
> Just put to rest all views.

It is a common misconception that Zen is about achieving inner
peace and tranquility. (That's why the name gets used to sell

perfumes, soaps, incense, and pillows.) In fact, Zen is about giving up all ideas and expectations about the way the world is or should be, including the expectation that enlightenment will eliminate one's sorrows. Nothing could be less Zenlike than the pursuit of tranquility. As one monk said on "coming to a realization," "Now that I'm enlightened, I'm just as miserable as ever."

It is a different kind of misery, of course. There would hardly be a reason to spend all those hours sitting if it weren't. But what enlightenment *feels like* is something that nobody can really communicate. As the *Xinxinming* says,

> If your eyes are open
> Dreams will naturally cease.
> If the mind makes no distinctions,

> ***

> As all grounds for distinction vanish,
> Nothing can be compared or described.

What we can say, though, is that life has a taste that is far more intense than that of the dreamworld where most of us spend our lives. It's the way the world first appeared to the great seventeenth-century poet and cleric Thomas Traherne:

> The corn was orient and immortal wheat, which never should be reaped, nor was ever sown. I thought it had stood from everlasting to everlasting. The dust and stones of the street were as precious as gold: the gates were at first the end of the world. The green trees when I saw them first through one of the gates transported and ravished me, their sweetness and unusual beauty made my heart to leap, and almost mad with ecstasy, they were such strange and wonderful things. The Men! O what venerable and reverend creatures did the aged seem! Immortal Cherubims! And young men glittering and sparkling Angels, and maids strange seraphic pieces of life and beauty! Boys and girls tumbling in the street, and playing, were moving jewels. I knew not that they were born or should die; But all things abided eternally as they were in their proper places.[17]

The condition of such magnificence, though, is that we give up our reliance in theories and facts altogether and embrace suffering and joy with the same selflessness: "Hold not to likes and dislikes!"

The Islamic mystical orders that we collectively call Sufism take a similar attitude toward the gap between ideas and reality. In one Sufi tale, a madman calls a muezzin's recitation of the 99 names of God "shaking an empty nutshell"; "How can God be understood through names?" he asks. "Since you cannot speak in words about the essence of God, better you speak of nobody at all."[18] In the words of another sage, "To be a Sufi is to put away what is in your head—imagined truth, preconceptions, conditioning—and to face what may happen to you."

In Farid ud-Din Attar's allegorical poem *The Conference of the Birds*, a favorite since the twelfth century, the birds who go in search of their king, the Simurgh, pass through seven dreadful valleys where the illusions of ordinary life drop off one by one. The meaning of each stage is revealed by the hoopoe, the birds' leader and guide. The fifth valley is the valley of unity, and in it the hoopoe tells this tale:

> An old woman offered Bu Ali a piece of gold saying: "Accept this from me." He replied, "I can accept things only from God." The old woman retorted, "Where did you learn to see double? You are not a man of power to bind and unbind. If you were not squint-eyed would you see several things at once?"[19]

The point, of course, is that there is no separation between the old woman and God himself.

When the 30 birds who persevere reach the king's palace, they discover that they are themselves merely aspects of the Simurgh. (This is a pun; "Simurgh" means "30 birds.") They are God, each other, and nobody at the same time:

> At last, in a state of contemplation, they realized that they were the Simurgh and that the Simurgh was the thirty birds. When they gazed at the Simurgh they saw that it was truly the Simurgh who was there,

and when they turned their eyes towards themselves they saw that
they themselves were the Simurgh. And perceiving both at once,
themselves and Him, they realized that they and the Simurgh were
one and the same thing. No one in the world has ever heard of anything to equal it.[20]

As the avian pilgrims now understand, the Simurgh cannot be separated from themselves, and they cannot be separated from the
Simurgh. But every possible idea they could frame about themselves
and the Simurgh had to disappear before they could come to see this.
As Attar wrote in his invocation,

> The knowledge of Him is not at the door of rhetoricians. Knowledge
> and ignorance are here the same, for they cannot explain nor can they
> describe. The opinions of men on this arise only in their imagination;
> and it is absurd to try to deduce anything from what they say: whether
> ill or well, they have said it from themselves. God is above knowledge
> and beyond evidence, and nothing can give an idea of his Holy Majesty.[21]

It is easy to spot the differences between *The Conference of the Birds*
and the *Xinxinming*. In its own fashion, Sufi thought is true to
Islamic monotheism, though Attar, at least, often strongly echoes
the tantra of Hinduism and Buddhism. The Sufis also share the
sense of human sinfulness found in all three Western traditions,
but rare or nonexistent in China and Japan. But with the climactic
revelation that the Simurgh and the kingdom of birds are one and
the same, the surface differences begin to fade.

What these diverse voices share is found within every religious tradition, Christianity not excepted, and it's a good starting point for a working understanding of religious activity that sidesteps the post-Christian
pitfalls of Dennett's and Dawkins's definitions. It is not a complicated
definition, and I think that it more or less appears on its own once we
stop expecting religion in general to be Christianity writ large.

Religious activities don't square with conscious thinking. They
undercut it. They wean us away from the ways in which the world

appears to us and the ways in which we experience our own inner lives. The world is not what it seems, and we do not know ourselves. What we take to be life is a shadow play, and behind or within it there is another world that alone can be considered real. We can experience that real world, but we can never say anything about it, and our facts never bring us any closer to it.

By "another world," I do not mean heaven or the pedestrian paradise on earth depicted in *Awake* or *The Watchtower*. Religious practices do not upgrade our surroundings. They work changes in the way we experience and feel. The world we encounter in religious practice is the real world just as it is, and once we touch that reality we realize that the realm of ordinary experience is the fantasy, concocted of our fears and hopes instead of anything solid. This is how even Christianity works. In the end, its articles of faith are meant to push the believer past the everyday, to see this very world as charged with the grandeur of God. In Zen and Christianity, as in indigenous religions, Sufism, Hinduism, Taoism, and so many others, the promise of religious discipline is contact with reality and a more profoundly true and abundant life.

It is not possible to describe reality. As soon as it is translated into words or images it becomes a story, nothing more than another fragment of the unreal life that we are trying to see beyond. The temptation to speak about what one has come to see is great, but yielding to it produces the monstrosities of institutionalized faith. In the words of the fourteenth-century Sufi sage Alauddin Attar,

> All religion, as theologians—and their opponents—understand the word, is something other than what it is assumed to be.
>
> Religion is a vehicle. Its expressions, rituals, moral and other teachings are designed to cause certain elevating effects, at certain times, upon certain communities.
>
> Because of the difficulty of maintaining the science of man, religion was instituted as a means of approaching truth. The means always became, for the shallow, the end, and the vehicle became the idol.

Only the man of wisdom, the man of faith or intellect, can cause the vehicle to move again.[22]

This is the great error of theology, of whatever variety.

The traditions do suggest, though, that there is an incomprehensible unity to the world and that all things within it move with an effortlessness that we ourselves can approach in those moments when the noise of discourse and inner monologue fall silent. To catch sight of this is not to leave reality behind; it is the real world we sense, and it is always there to support the everyday world of conscious experience. It is not an attainment, either, because the desire to reach reality is the greatest obstacle to encountering it. In the words of a famous Sufi saying, it is not found by seeking, but only seekers find it.

Reality is there, as plain as anything, but—as the poet Rumi said—nobody can show it to you; it is "hidden, and hidden, and hidden." As Jesus kept telling his uncomprehending listeners, "The kingdom of heaven is within you." It did most of his audience no good, of course; 2,000 years later, most Christians are still awaiting the arrival of what Jesus knew was as unobtrusive as a mustard seed and, like the leaven in bread, both everywhere and nowhere at once. And yet the message is there in Christianity as well if one knows where to look, and it has flowered through the millennia in visions like Traherne's.

We are so used to conventional ideas of reality and religion that all this may sound like mysticism. Many so-called mystics have shared these ideas, it's true, but there's nothing specifically mystical about them. They turn out to be shared by a lot of biologists and neurologists who haven't a mystical or theological thought in their heads. As their work is showing us, our conscious experience of the world really is a poor guide to the way the world works. It's like a bad movie version of real life. Our innermost thoughts and feelings have something fallacious about them. They are fragments masquerading as the whole.

Behind all the blather in our heads is something else: a comprehensive, profoundly unified web of interactions where there is neither you nor I and where even the differences between humans and other animals vanish. Because of the oddities of consciousness and of reflective thought, all this is truly "hidden, and hidden, and hidden." But it is not unavailable. For tens of thousands of years, people have learned and taught ways to catch sight of that order of things and to move in harmony with it. Reason and science cannot do as much; they, too, are only stories, though they are often useful and reasonably accurate ones. What they *can* show us, though, is that there's nothing imaginary about the world that spiritual practices lead us toward and nothing delusional in those moments of grace when all things work for the good.

Notes

1. Luke 15:18–19.
2. Luke 15:20–24.
3. I Corinthians 15:14.
4. Romans 7:18–20.
5. Romans 6:3–7.
6. Walter Burkert, *Homo necans: The anthropology of ancient Greek sacrificial ritual and myth*, trans. Peter Bing (Berkeley: University of California Press, 1983), 2.
7. Romans 10:9–10.
8. Burton Mack, *A myth of innocence: Mark and Christian origins* (Minneapolis: Fortress Press, 2006).
9. "Accident" in *The Catholic encyclopedia*, vol. 1 (New York: Appleton, 1913), 97.
10. Talal Asad, *Formations of the secular: Christianity, Islam, modernity* (Stanford, CA: Stanford University Press, 2003), 37–38. This aspect of medieval religion has been elucidated brilliantly by Caroline Walker Bynum.
11. Asad, *Formations of the secular: Christianity, Islam, modernity*, 38.
12. As every televangelist's show demonstrates, the conversion experience itself is still central to many forms of Protestantism.

13. Cicero, *De Oratore*, vol. 1, trans. E. W. Sutton and H. Rackham (Cambridge, MA: Harvard University Press: 1942): 325, bk. II, xlii, 178.

14. Translated by the Chung Tai Translation Committee, Chung Tai Zen Center of Sunnyvale, http://ctzen.org/sunnyvale/enUS/index.php?option=com_content&task=view&id=143&Itemid=57.

15. These concepts are hardly ever separated in Chinese thought anyway, which does not use our metaphors of head and heart and takes thinking and feeling to be identical products of the *xin*, or "heart/mind."

16. R. H. Blyth, *Zen and Zen classics*, vol. 1 (Boston: Shambhala Publications, 2005), 71–72.

17. Thomas Traherne, *Centuries of meditation*, ed. Bertram Dobell (London: B. Dobell, 1908), 156–57.

18. Idries Shah, *The way of the Sufi* (New York: Dutton, 1970), 66.

19. Farid ud-Din Attar, *The conference of the birds*, trans. S. C. Nott (London: Continuum, 2000), 130.

20. Attar, *The conference of the birds*, 147.

21. Attar, *The conference of the birds*, 14–15.

22. Shah, *The way of the Sufi*, 239.

4

Every Body Is a Mind of Its Own

To start with a question: What might it mean to say, with Darwin, that "the mind is a function of body"? Darwin himself may not have meant anything startling, of course; we could look at it as a simple claim that everything mental can be explained in terms of biology. This would not have been such an unusual thought even for Darwin's day. But he could easily be saying something else. He might be suggesting that we can't draw a line between the two. What we think of as "mind" and what we think of as "body" are not separate. Ultimately they're one and the same.

This raises some very intriguing possibilities, but it seems to run up against the obvious facts of experience. Mind and body are self-evidently two different kinds of things. The mind looks like something special. It's active and creative in a unique way. We feel ourselves to be alive with purpose and with free will, possessed of a universe of deeply personal hopes and ambitions, and our sense of what it is to be a human being in a real world seems to depend on these feelings. The mind is where all this seems to take place. We think of it as the seat of our very soul or whatever it is that we want to call the source of our individuality and identity. The body, on the other hand, feels like something we have, not something we are. It seems like an instrument, a mere thing. It doesn't think; it gets thought *about*. It rumbles and prods, and parts of it seem to have minds of their own, but most of the time it sits around waiting for directions. Without the mind or the soul it would be nothing. Many of us feel that our selves could walk away from their bodies altogether without losing anything essential, and while there's no reason to think that we really could do this, the persistence of this notion says a lot about the way we experience and think of ourselves.

How could mind be a function of this kind of body? How could a thing become a "me"? The short answer is that it isn't and it doesn't. Neither the body nor the mind is the way we think of it. "Mind" and "body" are produced by our very attempt to make sense of our experience, and they have no separate existence outside this attempt. We are not split in two.

Yet we do separate them. We can't help ourselves. No matter how much we try, we seem to have no way of shaking the sense that mind and body come from two different worlds and are made up of two different substances. Darwin's note suggests that we look behind that belief and figure out where it comes from. That seems like a good way to set out.

What do we do when we try to make sense of experience, and how does that hand us the split between mind and body? You can start to see the answer by thinking about what you do whenever you think about anything. Whatever you think about—cats, walls, books, apples, jars of horseradish, your husband or wife, a goddess, the sound of a conch shell being sounded at a Hindu temple, or a pair of tangerines on the desk beside your computer—every act of thinking has one common characteristic. In every single thought, *you* are the *subject* of your thoughts, and the things that you think about are the *objects* of those thoughts. Whenever you act as a thinking subject, everything else becomes an object. As the author of the *Xinxinming* wrote,

> Objects are objects because of subjects,
> Subjects are subjects because of objects.

This is a very important insight. It explains why the body feels passive and objectlike when we think about it. It has to be passive, a mere thing, simply because whenever you're aware of it, you're thinking about it, *and thinking about anything makes it into a thing.*

Things, even sophisticated complex things like "that wonderful machine, our body," have no initiative, creativity, or intentionality, and they certainly don't have hopes and dreams and longings. Those are properties of the subject, the mind.[1] If we encounter anyone or anything that has those characteristics, we assume that these things, too, are inhabited and managed by minds.

All this seems reasonable and even obvious. As philosophers have pointed out, though, things just aren't as simple as that, and if you try to think this way about your own mind you start to get into trouble. Give it a try—think about your mind. What's doing the thinking when you do that? Your mind, is, of course, because the mind is the subjective part of your experience. As soon as you think about it, though, the mind is no longer subjective. It's an object—a thing.

This is the problem. "Mind" turns out to be the name you use when you think of your subjective activity. You can't give it a name and think about that activity, though, without turning it into an object, thanks to the rule that anything that you think about has got to be an object of your thoughts. So the mind is essentially subjective life seen as an object. It's a subject and an object at the same time—but you can never actually experience it that way. Every time you think of the mind, you make it un-mind-like; you turn your subjective life into something that isn't subjective at all.

This is so confusing that we could spend a few hundred pages discussing the problems it raises. We're not likely to reach any conclusions, though—and that may be for the best. Instead of trying to solve these all-but-insoluble problems, we might be better off if we took them as signs that our everyday notions of mind and body are leading us astray.

So let's try to steer clear of imagining ourselves as free, active minds in charge of passive, mechanical bodies. Once we do that we will start seeing the world in a different way. We discover that living, active bodies act mindfully even if they lack anything that looks like a mind or anyplace where a mind might find a home—a brain, for instance. All bodies, from the simplest bacteria on up, are open, sensitive, responsive, and filled with information. All of them are knowledgeable and purposeful in the same way that we imagine the mind to be.

This is not simply because these bodies were stocked with instincts and other "programs" coded into their genes. Bodies learn things, too. The very structure of our flesh and bone is made through a process of learning, and even now, as you read this, parts of you are being remade without any mind intervening or any nerve cells, either.

One more caution before we set out. Just as we can't say "religion" and think "Christianity," we need to avoid the mistake of saying "brain" and thinking "mind." That's a common problem in itself; we've already seen that Dawkins's and Dennett's "brain" is little more than another name for the mind. It may look like we're explaining mental life by pointing to a special part of the body, but if you step back for a moment, you can see that we really haven't explained anything at all. We've just taken the division between mind and body and turned it into one between brain and "rest of body." We're still left with no idea of how the thoughts that whiz around inside us are related to the gray and white stuff in our skulls.

So let us keep temptation far from our door. We'll ignore the brain and the entire nervous system and make *this* chapter, at least, a nerve-free zone. We'll look at nothing more than bodies without nerve cells. The nervous system can have a chapter of its own on the condition that it stay out of this one.

Let us start, then, with the simplest bacteria, creatures with no nerves, no brain, and nothing much else, either. Some bacteria have tails, or flagellae, that move them around. But we want nothing so advanced. The bacteria we're interested in are little more than bags of chemical soup inside a casing. The soup is called cytoplasm, and in it floats the bacterium's DNA. There is no nucleus and no other organelles in "prokaryotes" like these—just soup, casing, and a loop of DNA.

These bacteria are nothing much to look at, then, but they're definitely alive. They eat, excrete, grow, and reproduce. Their simplicity conceals an array of complex systems, as biologist Lynn Margulis writes:

> The most stripped-down minimal form of life on Earth is still extraordinarily complex. Just a tiny membrane-bounded sphere, a wall-less bacterial cell requires a cadre of molecular interactions, more than fifteen kinds of DNA and RNA, [and at least] . . . five hundred different types of protein . . . usually closer to five thousand kinds.[2]

The casing is a perfect example of this. What looks to the most powerful of microscopes like a simple membrane is itself a miracle of miniaturized complexity. Different species of bacteria get their nutrition from different chemicals, and their waste products vary just as widely. That's why some are so useful, like the lactobacilli that turn milk into yogurt, and others are so deadly. Each bacterium is equipped with specialized molecular pumps that filter out the chemicals that it finds useless or toxic and that admit only those that it needs. Other pumps run in reverse, taking out the trash while keeping the good stuff inside.

Other systems regulate the germ's shape and size. Embedded in its membrane are molecules that work like the iris diaphragm of a camera lens. If the organism begins to swell because its internal pressure is too high, the cell membrane stretches and these coils open, creating a little porthole in the cell wall. As soon as some excess cytoplasm leaks out, the internal pressure goes down. The coils close up, and the germ returns to normal.

Every organism devotes much of its time to tasks like these. None can survive without maintenance systems, without systems that ingest and process food, and without a system to expel waste. All these systems work together to preserve the organism's internal structure. What's more, all of them need to respond to the world outside. Living is a matter of balancing inner structure with a changing environment, and each system keeps in touch with the outside world and works tirelessly to keep its organism's inner state within safe limits. Biologists call this maintaining homeostasis.[3] Thanks to the need to maintain homeostasis, every living thing is always coordinating its actions with the world outside.

The homeostatic systems in bacteria don't suggest mental life at all. They're mechanical processes, and it's perfectly reasonable to suppose that all the directions for those wonderfully sophisticated cell membranes are safely written down in its DNA. But even the simplest germ is nothing like the broomstick charmed by the sorcerer's apprentice, running a single-minded program as it drifts around and soaks up the goodies that surround it.[4] Instead, bacteria do different things in different surroundings. Their DNA contain recipes for proteins that fit a range of activities, and in different environments germs will order up different proteins to respond effectively and flourish in each particular setting.

Such responsiveness to the environment means that these organisms "know" things. They don't think about their internal pressure or wonder which molecules they would like to assimilate next, but their activity is so connected with their surroundings that we can find out something about the environment simply by looking at what the bacteria are doing. No matter how simple it may be, *every organism acts as if it's aware of the world outside its skin.*

Look, for instance, at the spectacular ways in which bacteria grow and reproduce. When a single bacterium is put into the microscopic equivalent of an all-you-can-eat buffet, such as a scientist's Petri dish with its highly nutritious agar-agar, it grows and multiplies until the whole dish is covered with its descendants. This isn't a simple process, though. Instead, the bacterium adjusts its internal workings several times. It isn't generally ready to eat so well or be so fecund, so it can't dig in right away. It has to prepare for the feast to come and for the orgy of growth that follows, and after it's finished it has to recover and get back to the more tedious chores of everyday life.

Once it encounters the nutrients, then, the bacterium concocts special proteins from its DNA's store of recipes, ones that aren't used most of the time but that are essential to growing and multiplying. Only when everything is in order does it pass from this "lag phase" into the "log phase" of rapid growth, where its population of descendants can double in as little as 10 to 20 minutes.[5]

Then, after the new mats of bacteria have eaten up most of the nutrients, the bacteria move into a third phase, one of stabilization and a return to normal. Now their metabolism is throttled back. Specialized subsystems check over their DNA and repair any errors, ensuring that the internal protein recipes are still good. Antioxidants circulate to mop up the harmful substances that piled up inside during the riotous expansion of the log phase.

In growth and reproduction, then, bacteria undertake a surprisingly complex set of processes, constantly checking both internal and external states. Both determine what they will do next. The signal for the log phase of explosive growth is generated from within; reproduction doesn't start until the organism is ready. At the same time, though, the entire process is regulated by feedback from outside. A high concentration of nutrients starts it off, and a decline in the nutrient concentration will slow and then stop that same process.

Germs have no minds, but they know things about their world. They do not get a whiff of the agar plate and think, "Wowee! Pastures of plenty!" But they would not behave very differently if they did, and it is not playing with words to call this knowledge. Knowledge isn't limited to ideas that we can write down or explain to someone else. There's something else that we recognize as knowledge, and where this kind of knowledge is concerned, we're not as different from the germ world as we might like to think we are.

When we learn how to play music or bake bread, for instance, we don't memorize a list of rules and definitions that add up to those skills. We don't learn *what* to do. We learn *how* to do them, which is why we call it "know-*how*." This doesn't lead to new conscious knowledge in our heads, and we don't pick these practices up by instruction or memorization. Instead, we put our bodies to work practicing new skills, and we realize that we have these skills when we feel ourselves acting in new ways. This is the kind of knowledge that lets us play a page of Schubert with accuracy and feeling or know when the fish is done or sense from the consistency of dough that we can stop kneading. Know-how is implicit, *embodied* knowledge rather than the overt, reflective knowledge that we get from a book, but it's real knowledge all the same, even though we can't reduce it to a list of facts or theories and rarely have any access to it at all.[6]

We all accept that this is real knowledge. Imagine that someone tells you that she's learned to play the piano. Maybe you think she's be pulling your leg, so you ask her to prove it. Your friend could do a good many things by way of a response, but the one thing that she's *not* going to do is pull out a sheet of music paper, point to some notes, and say, "When you see this one, you press the D below middle C. *This one* means that you press the F-sharp above C above middle C, very quickly," and so on. She's not going to tell you any fact that she's memorized or any information that she's acquired. Instead, of course, the best way for her to convince you that she's telling the truth is to sit down at a piano and *play* something. (In fact, you're as likely to say "Show me" to her as anything else, so this is the answer you expected all along.)

When someone starts learning the piano, it's true, they usually have to learn the names of the notes, their locations on the piano keyboard, and how those sounds are specified in musical notation. But they forget the notes when they've memorized the piece, and once they've learned to sight-read music, the proper hand and pedal movements happen spontaneously when they look at the score. Anything that goes on inside the player is completely unavailable to reflection. This is a good thing musically; if a pianist needed to think about what to do in order to play each note, she would never be able to play any but the simplest and slowest tunes.

You can tell from everyday language that we think of piano playing this way. Instead of saying, "I've only learned part of how to play the piano," we say, "I don't play the piano very well." We make the same distinction in many other fields, too. A teenager preparing for his driver's tests will say, "I've memorized half of the stuff in the driver's manual," but "My driving's pretty good except for parallel parking." We use these two different ways of talking because they point to two different forms of knowledge. The driver's manual lists the facts we need to know in order to pass the written driver's test. It's a compendium of conscious, reflective knowledge, and it can be memorized as a series of sentences. The skills of a competent driver, though, can be learned only by practice. You can't cram for the road test. You have to practice over and over because, unlike the written exam, the road test checks our embodied knowledge, our driving know-how.

Our advantage as humans, of course, is that we *can* learn to play the piano, drive a car, or bake bread. The bacterium can't learn anything at all. Its knowledge is fixed. This is a tremendously significant difference, and it should not be minimized. But that doesn't mean that what's implicit in the bacterium can't be called knowledge. Even though it seems infinitely far removed from the skills that we humans cultivate and possess, the bacterium's ability to adjust to its surroundings and make the best use of its environment can properly be called a form of knowledge, too.

This is supposed to be a nerve-free chapter, and our own ability to learn and our knowledge of the world and of ourselves depend very heavily on the nervous system. But this kind of knowledge didn't begin when animals first grew brains, and learning doesn't need brains or nerves, either. Consider the one-celled amoeba, the only animal that everyone can manage to draw.[7] Amoebas are much more complex than bacteria. Still, they're only single cells, and they're as bereft of nerves and brain as any bacterium. Yet amoebas are talented creatures with a surprising range of abilities.

Amoebas act intentionally, just like you and me. In other words, their activity can be focused on a moment-to-moment basis toward something else. In their case, this is generally food. They're omnivores of a sort, living off smaller protozoans as well as algae, and they can draw on a number of hunting techniques. Here is a description from a talented amateur biologist:

> The cytoplasm inside the cell is capable of changing into different states. It can turn very easily from a fluid into a solid state and vice versa. The fluid state of the cytoplasm is called plasmasol, the more solid state is called plasmagel. When the organism locomotes the plasmasol flows through the center of the cell towards the front. When the plasmasol moves to the sides it becomes solid again. This way the cell can propel itself as a whole but can also send pseudopodia in many directions.
>
> It is this pseudopodia movement that enables the amoeba to capture prey. Usually the pseudopods form a kind of 'dome' that makes escaping impossible. They have to have some sort of chemical detection since they notice prey without having to touch it. Amoebas seem to use different engulfing tactics to suit the various types of prey. They can detect if a prey needs a fast approach (ciliates) or can be feasted on as a slow meal (immobile algae).[8]

These are only a few of their abilities. Amoebas can vary the stickiness of their outer membrane in order to glide along surfaces. They have a front and a back, although these look the same to us. In a hostile environment like the human body, the amoeba that causes dysentery will clean off the telltale surface proteins that mark it as an intruder and push them off its back end, thus evading the host's immune system.

Most surprising of all, amoebas can learn and remember things. If you take a tiny needle and poke one in the front, it will change direction. Poke it in the back, and it will move away. But if you keep prodding it from behind, it will gradually stop responding. It's become *habituated* to the touch of the needle, and it no longer changes behavior when it feels that touch.[9]

It's a stretch to call this full-fledged learning, but habituation is a big step along the path that leads to learning itself. The amoeba normally tries to flee an unfamiliar stimulus. The advantage of this response is obvious; it's much more likely that the stimulus indicates danger rather than food. But every move costs the amoeba precious energy, so it makes equal evolutionary sense for it to ignore any unusual stimulus that's *not* connected with a threat. Habituation reconciles these two strategies. It's a way of changing behavior once the unexpected turns out not to be the unfortunate.

You can't get habituated, though, unless you can recognize that the second, third, and fourth stimuli are the same as the first. You have to compare them with one another. The other stimuli aren't present any more, though, and they can't be experienced directly. Instead, they have to be summoned up and set alongside the present stimulus to see if they match.

Because amoebas can become habituated, we have to assume that they "remember" if a stimulus is one that they've encountered before. The amoeba is thus connecting the needle prick it's feeling right now with several needle pricks that it felt in the past. This is a complex task, and it demands some capabilities that we would never expect of a mere body, let alone one as primitive as an amoeba's.

I'm not suggesting that amoebas have the kind of conscious memory that we have, and it would be a stretch to say that the amoeba "thinks." But it not only knows things about the environment, it can also add to the things that it knows and keep them in, do we dare say, mind? The amoeba seems to know a great deal, and it moves and acts with direction and purpose, all without nerves, sensory organs, or any obvious internal structure. There is probably no better demonstration that knowledge and intentionality, key parts of our notion of mind, are characteristics of the simplest of bodies.

But it's really a mistake to call the amoeba simple. The structure of a nucleated cell—a "eukaryote"—is highly complex. Like other eukaryotes, amoebas have nuclei and mitochondria, centrioles, and many other smaller parts and substructures. (The technical term for these is organelles.) And it's now well accepted that many of these organelles descend from specialized bacteria that joined forces in mutually beneficial cooperation.

The single cell of an amoeba is actually a community, and its cell membrane is more like a protective wall around a village—with guards at its gates—than anything else. This partnership goes back to the first stirrings of life.[10] The earliest "anaerobic" bacteria thrived in the hot, acid, oxygen-free environment of the early earth. Oxygen was poison to them. We ourselves couldn't live without this element, but oxygen is a highly dangerous gas because so many elements combine with it. That is why we encase precious documents in nitrogen-filled cases, paint metal so it won't rust, and take antioxidants in hopes of keeping ourselves healthy.

The oxygen-free paradise of the early earth didn't last, however. Other bacteria developed photosynthesis, the trick of living off solar energy, and these new green bacteria multiplied rapidly. As we all know, one waste product of photosynthesis is oxygen. The green bacteria were more efficient than their ancestors—they were harnessing solar energy directly—and they began pumping oxygen into the atmosphere at an alarming rate.

This first of many biological transformations of the earth posed a giant challenge for oxygen-hating species. A few of their distant descendants survive in the vents of volcanoes and other places that the rest of us would find inhospitable. Most anaerobic life, though, either died off or took shelter. The lucky ones entered into partnership with other organisms with cell walls that could tolerate the increasing levels of oxygen. Inside the safety of the cell wall, the anaerobic bacteria could survive—not as independent organisms but as organelles doing jobs that the rest of the cell found useful.

The most important step forward for these symbiotic communities was incorporating yet other bacteria that could take advantage of oxygen's dangerous tendency to combine with other elements. These miniature powerhouses mixed oxygen with other elements to generate lots of energy. They were the ancestors of our mitochondria. Their talent for generating energy from oxygen, carbon, and hydrogen gave these new complex cells a huge evolutionary advantage over simpler organisms.

When we think about the lowly amoeba, then, we should imagine a dizzying number of interactions among parts that themselves incorporate a wide range of responses. If a simple bacterium can have 5,000 different proteins used in different ways, we can imagine how much complexity comes about when several different kinds of bacteria operate together within a single eukaryotic cell. The amoeba's success, then, depends on the constant interplay of the community inside its membrane. Like every cell, it is a miracle of coordination. The descendants of formerly independent bacteria retain the complexity and responsiveness that they had on their own, but all these different systems, each responding to all the others, are now coordinated with one another and with the environment to maintain the homeostasis of their one-cell village.

When we get to multicellular organisms, these interrelationships get infinitely more complicated. It's hard not to think of our compact, strongly bounded body as a single thing, but we should realize that it's equally valid to see it as a huge colony of colonies of bodies, a vast federal union of single-celled animals, each cell with its own embodied knowledge and each made up of its own community of responsive and knowledgeable organelles.

Every one of us is plural, even multiply plural. We inhabit—no, we *are*—nations in ourselves, like the man on the title page of Thomas Hobbes's *Leviathan* whose huge body is made of innumerable tiny people. The body that looks simple and single to our eyes and to our imagination is an array of different groups of cells. Each group has its own function, and each one seeks its own ends. Some cells get on very well with their neighbors, while others struggle for survival; very often, a group that builds something up is paired with another that tears it down. Among the white blood corpuscles or leukocytes, which can sense and identify prey, are macrophages, long-lived cells that are almost like amoebas who've cast their lot in with the rest of us, blobby predators who rove our body and gobble up things that shouldn't be there. We even host a population of immigrant workers, trillions of bacteria that we rely on to help us digest our food and perform many other tasks.[11]

A large multicellular organism is something of a world made up of worlds. This is something more than a metaphor. Animals like ourselves—and plants, too—are cooperative undertakings through which a large number of single-celled organisms carry their ideal environment with them. We are walking aquariums. Our eukaryotic ancestors lived in the ocean, so it's not surprising that the chemical composition of the human body is very close to that of seawater. These primitive organisms preferred warmth, and we keep our internal temperature at a balmy 37 degrees Celsius. They needed food and dissolved oxygen in the water, and their descendants inside you and me are treated to a steady flow of nutrients and oxygen. Organelles thrive in the controlled environment of the interior of a cell, which preserves the oxygen-poor environment they came out of. In the same way, our individual cells thrive in a body whose interior conditions mimic the warm tropical oceans where *they* first evolved.

The homeostatic work of a bacterium or an amoeba is keeping its own internal organization in good order and fueling itself so that it has the energy it needs for its primary job. The cells in our own body have the same internal maintenance task—otherwise, they would die—but they work two jobs, not one. Their "outside" job is maintaining the internal order and conditions of the whole multicellular organism that they make up. They need to keep the aquarium clean, and they need it to obtain and ingest food.

From the cells' perspective, our internal state is the "outer" environment, just like the pond is for the amoeba and the agar plate is for the laboratory bacterium and just like the interior of a cell is for the organelles. But these environments aren't created and maintained by outside forces like the pond or the Petri dish are. They're produced by the cells themselves as they respond to one another. For any given cell, the "outside world" is produced by the joint activity of it and all the other cells in the body. Paradoxically, *our cells are one another's environment.*

This degree of interdependence requires very close coordination. If Dawkins and Dennett were correct, there ought to be some superdetailed set of instructions that assigns each cell to its proper place in the body and constantly tells it what to do. Yet every cell in the body has the same DNA. It's pretty hard to imagine how this could direct each cell's specific activities and manage the organism as a whole at the same time. In fact, there is no evidence at all that multicellular organisms are top-down dictatorships. Instead, they appear to be cooperative undertakings that rely on countless peer-to-peer interactions.

The cells of a multicellular organism can't use a master programmer or a book of instructions. Instead, they respond to the environment, as every organism does—only the environment is the product of their own activity and that of all their compatriots added together. Each cell's actions ripple out and affect all the others in turn, setting up a slightly different internal environment that now calls for slightly different activity on the part of all the cells, the first one included. Cause and effect shuttle back and forth. Imagine the millions of cells in a single human body woven together through their sensitivity to each other's activities, and you begin to grasp the complexity of our bodily life and the source of our incredible physical resilience and adaptability.

This can't be explained by DNA alone; as we've already noted, every one of the cells in an organism has the same DNA. Individual cells don't follow directions, carry blueprints of the entire body, or monitor news bulletins to figure out what needs to be done next. They respond to signals from other cells, usually the ones closest by. Their embodied knowledge of what other cells are doing factors into their actions, and it's broadcast through those actions to the rest of the community, to be incorporated into every cell's knowledge. Through constant multidimensional and multidirectional feedback, all the body's cells link their activities with all the others, ceaselessly responding to those that are responding to them. Just because this coordination is horizontal and not top down, it depends crucially on each cell's sensitivity to its surroundings and the flexibility of its response. We could not survive in an ever-changing world otherwise.

The sophistication of the genetic code, then, isn't the only thing that keeps us alive. What counts as much or even more is the openness of one cell to another. This coordination through feedback is found everywhere, from the interior of individual cells to the balancing act that a population carries out with the rest of its ecosystem.

The very shape and structure of our bodies, in fact, is built through such feedback loops. We very literally incorporate our past. One surprising example involves the useful but dangerous mineral calcium. Calcium is essential to muscle action, but contrary to what you might assume from all the calcium supplements being advertised, too much of it is toxic waste. Cells long ago developed pumps to keep excess calcium out. Multicellular organisms have to excrete it.

In the primitive oceans (as in today's oceans, too) this calcium waste came in contact with chemicals and turned into hard minerals: calcium phosphate and calcium carbonate. About 540 million years ago, some organisms took advantage of this fact. They started spreading their calcium secretions around them, where it solidified into protective shells.[12]

This security came with a price, however. Most of these organisms were either stuck in place by their calcium-rich fortifications or found moving around difficult. Eventually, a new twist developed: animals started to turn this part of themselves inside out. Instead of making shells with their excess calcium, they imported phosphates and began building bones with the combination. Internal skeletons gave them a tremendous advantage. The combination of stiffness and flexibility helped them outswim almost every invertebrate that ever existed, and vertebrates were able to grow larger without any loss of mobility.[13] The giant squid excepted, all the most advanced forms of life need their bones. All of them depend on recycling waste calcium.

Our bones and teeth are made the same way, and as a result, calcium is the most common mineral in the human body. But this doesn't mean that the body got rid of its calcium patrol. In fact, our bodies retain osteocytes, which use calcium to build bones, and osteoclasts, which dissolve calcium so that it can be excreted. Both of these are constantly at work. As a result, our bones are always under attack and demand constant maintenance.

This seems like a terrible waste, but it's no such thing. It's yet another way of adjusting to the environment. As physiologist J. Scott Turner writes,

> Bones do not start out elegantly built. . . . That comes about when the bone is adaptively remodeled, which draws on the rivalry between the besieged osteocytes and the pillaging osteoclasts. Normally, the osteoclasts are held at bay by a protective layer of protein that envelopes the bone's mineral layers. That changes if events—irritation, injury, or something else—strips this protein layer away, exposing the mineral. Then osteoclasts swarm in, like Mongols into a breached fortification, plowing up the mineralized matrix, the supporting foundation of collagen, cartilage, and blood vessels, ultimately displacing the osteocytes. . . . Adaptive remodeling begins once the osteoclasts finish their grim work and move on. . . . [M]icrofractures of individual . . . cylinders are always occurring within bone, and this means that the bone is continually being plowed up, resettled, and rebuilt. . . . Repeated again and again, this remodeling process gradually brings the . . . cylinders into alignment with the prevailing strain.[14]

Osteocytes and osteoclasts balance each other out. Because of that delicate balance, a very small input from elsewhere can shift the balance point and change the shape of our skeletons. Here, too, we can see the advantage of coordination by feedback over top-down planning. Because the seemingly solid bone is always being rebuilt, it can be reshaped to cope with the specific stresses that it has to face as the skeleton of a particular individual living a particular life in a particular place.

No genetic program could sculpt bones in advance to cope with an individual's unique experiences. It could only "engineer" a general purpose skeleton that could survive most conditions. To be ready for anything, though, it would have to be big and heavy. No such fail-safe structure could serve as well as a custom-made skeleton that adjusts to change. Its weight would hamper mobility, and the over-sized muscles needed to move it would demand more food. An animal with this kind of off-the-rack design would be an evolutionary dud.

It's a mistake, then, to think of organisms as little machines set loose in an alien environment. They are deeply embraided with one another and with their world. What they are and what they do can't be teased out from the larger network, the web of coordination that they—and we—shape as it shapes all of us. Our bodies, like the smallest bacteria, resonate with the whole system of which they are parts. Our bones record the stresses we face as we walk each day. Our lungs reflect the conditions of the atmosphere and how much and in what way we exercise.

These adjustments are parts of genuine feedback loops because other organisms experience our own activity as parts of *their* environment. Each organism changes in each encounter, and the nature of each encounter is shaped by the history of each organism. We coordinate our activity with one another and move in and out of harmony with one another, yet we do this without any overall plan and direction. Our bodies themselves bring us together.

Commonsense ideas about the body are wrong, then. It is not a static tool or a machine brilliantly laid out and ready for whatever needs to be done. It is changeable and full of knowledge, transformed by its history and by what it learns along the way. We write our autobiography in the flesh and respond with all our embodied knowledge, and for all that we are bounded by skin and hair and seemingly cut off from everything else, our bodies are open to the world. Their motions resonate with those of all living things.

It should not seem so strange, then, to think that mind is a function of this kind of body. As we shall see in the next chapter, much of what the brain does is merely an extension of those very same processes. Brains, too, are built for coordination instead of control, and they depend very heavily on the unconscious and unreachable knowledge of the rest of the body.

Notes

1. "What about other people?" you may ask, "aren't they subjects too?" We can't experience them as subjects, of course, unless we can pull off the Vulcan mind meld, but we certainly acknowledge them to be subjects just like us, and we treat them like that, which is a very good thing. It turns out to be a major puzzle to figure out why we're sure of this, however. We know other people only as objects, and we have no objective way to prove that everyone else isn't a cleverly constructed android. In philosophy, this is often called the "zombie problem," and you'll have to wait until Chapter 5 to read at least one solution to it.

2. Lynn Margulies, *Symbiotic planet: A new view of evolution* (New York: Basic Books, 1998), 82–83.

3. Because the optimal internal state will vary in cycles, like human body temperature does through the day, some people prefer the term "homeodynamics."

4. This is more the way viruses operate, and many biologists do not consider viruses to be alive.

5. For general background, see http://www.ifr.ac.uk/bacanova/project _backg.html. This means that you can go from one germ to a thousand

in a couple of hours, putting into perspective the claims that some spray disinfectants kill 99.9 percent of household germs.

6. Even people with short-term memory loss can learn this way, although they don't remember their teacher from one moment to the next.

7. Technically, amoebas are not animals, and many biologists today prefer to call them "protists." I use the word "animal," though, because the behavior of the amoeba is exactly what we'd expect of an animal, and it's their behavior that I want to focus on.

8. http://www.microscopy-uk.org.uk/mag/indexmag.html? http://www.microscopy-uk.org.uk/mag/artsep01/feed.html.

9. Habituation among amoebas has been observed and recorded for some time, at least since the work of J. D. Harris, "Habituatory response decrement in the intact organism," *Psychological Bulletin* 40 (1943): 385–422.

10. The following account is drawn largely from the work of Margulies, *Symbiotic planet*.

11. Current research suggests that intestinal flora affect our emotions and behavior, too. Mice raised in sterile conditions are dangerously incautious. Without the chemicals secreted by their intestinal bacteria, they don't have the instincts needed to avoid open areas where they can be picked off by birds; see K. Neufeld et al., "Reduced anxiety-like behavior and central neurochemical change in germ-free mice," *Neurogastroenterology and Motility* 23 (2011), doi:10.1111/j.1365-2982.2010.01620.x.

12. Galina T. Ushatinskaya, "Brachiopods," in *The ecology of the Cambrian radiation*, ed. A. Y. Zhuravlev and R. Riding (New York: Columbia University Press, 2001), 362; see also http://www.pbs.org/wgbh/evolution/change/deeptime/paleoz.html.

13. The exception is the squid, which developed a different internal structure from calcium carbonate.

14. J. Scott Turner, *The tinkerer's accomplice: How design emerges from life itself* (Cambridge, MA: Harvard University Press, 2007), 76–78.

5

I Don't Make the News, I Just Report It

We can ignore the nervous system only so long. It's pretty obvious that we would be nothing without our sense organs, our nerves, and our brain, and any account of life that left them out would be totally inadequate. Bodies may be extraordinarily responsive, and they might incorporate all kinds of knowledge, but without nerves there's only so much that they can know and do.

Remember, though, that we've been looking at living organisms from this angle because we're trying to challenge the idea that the body is a passive object run by a mental control center. We fall into that trap all the time because it's the way it feels to think and act as a self-conscious being. This may be the inevitable view "from the inside," but that doesn't mean that it's an accurate account of the way things work. We still have to keep our minds open, especially about the mind itself, and that means doubting even the most obvious aspects of experience.

We have good, rational, scientific reasons for doing this, but this kind of doubt is one of the unexpected things that scientific inquiry shares with religious practice. As we saw before, one thread that seems to run through all of religious life is that the way things appear to us isn't the way things really are. Science begins from something very similar. It tries to leave all possible questions open, testing out even the ideas that seem preposterous—and many ideas that seem self-evident today *did* sound preposterous at first. Great scientists had to fight against common sense to prove theories like the sun-centered order of the solar system and the germ theory of disease. "How could the earth be moving when it feels so solid beneath our feet?" they asked Copernicus. Louis Pasteur was confronted by scores of brilliant minds who wondered how tiny animals that nobody can see could make a grown man sick.

We can't do without common sense, but we can't take it too literally, either. It's only after a lot of research and questioning that we can see when it's reliable and when it leads us astray. Until then we have to doubt all our certainties. And the need to keep doubting is nowhere stronger than here, in the apparent connection between the concentration of nerve calls called the brain and the agile, fluid, free, and all-powerful mind that we find when we "look" inside ourselves. Let's not jump to any conclusions. It's better to proceed step-by-step.

The first question we need to ask is, Why do we have a nervous system when cells communicate very well through chemical signals? The answer is simple. Chemical signals work well enough for amoebas and other beings no bigger than a pencil dot and for communication within a small or coherent internal organ, but they'd be nobody's choice to coordinate an organism as big as a human being, a cat, or even an earthworm. There are simply too many cells that need to be contacted in these creatures, and very often the cells that need to be reached are far away. Chemical signals spread out in all directions, they get mixed up with other substances, and they get diluted quickly. What's more, they're relatively slow. Fast-moving creatures like cats and people face dangers that need immediate responses. You wouldn't want to rely on chemical signaling when you touch your finger to a hot stove; your whole finger might go up in smoke before a warning flag made it from the burning fingertip to the muscles that move the arm away.

Any organism with lots of cells needs communications channels that direct messages to the correct recipients. The endocrine system, for example, produces specialized signaling chemicals and sends them out along the bloodstream, piggybacking on a transportation infrastructure that had developed to carry food, oxygen, and waste products. Other chemical systems use dedicated ducts, not unlike the gas and water pipelines under city streets.

What we're interested in here, though, is the body's information superhighway, the nervous system. This is a surprisingly accurate metaphor because the nervous system runs off of electricity. It's a wired network, and its synapses are hardwired entry and exit ports like the Ethernet sockets in a hotel room or office. In the body, of course, the wiring isn't copper or fiber optics. Iit's made up of specialized cells called neurons instead. The most common neurons look like long threads with branches at both ends, very much like cables that sprouted. These threads are called axons, and the branches are called dendrites. Most dendrites have sensitive tips. These, the synapses, are the ports for the neuron. They're where the cell receives and transmits signals. Once triggered, a synapse sends a signal down through the dendrites and along the axon. When the signal reaches the other end, it sets a synapse at the far end to fire, thus passing the signal on to other neurons, to muscle cells, endocrine glands, or other groups of cells.

This is the simplest possible way for a neuron to operate, and it's likely that the first ones to evolve did just that, merely passing signals from one part of the organism to the other. This is the major function of primitive nervous systems, like those in sea slugs and the small tentacled hydra. These make do with a mesh of neurons in a grid, like chicken wire rolled into a tube.[1]

Complex neural nets can be very powerful, but a primitive one is useful for keeping all the cells "on the same page" and not much else. The hydra's net connects with photoreceptors and touch sensors, and it shuttles signals around so that the organism as a whole responds to light and touch. That's it. No brain is involved—the hydra has no brain. The net is there to facilitate peer-to-peer coordination among all the hydra's cells, something that would be impossible using chemical signals alone. But the hydra's nerves remain a kind of broadcast system, like chemical signaling only faster. Everyone gets the same message, so the hydra usually responds all over to a stimulus on one side.[2]

The hydra also has a ring of nerve cells at the top of its stalklike body.[3] These appear to connect with the tentacles, which are its main weapon and its organ for food gathering. This ring is selective in what it passes on, so it's the closest that the hydra gets to a brain, and it calls for specialized "smart" neurons like the ones that are the building blocks of all complex nervous systems and all brains. For not all nerve cells operate as simple transmitters. Some reverse the signal they receive—that is, an outside signal will make them stop transmitting. Other synapses will add signals together and transmit only when the sum of the signals reaches a certain threshold. When these specialized neurons are combined, the nervous system becomes a processor as well as a carrier of signals.

How powerful can a system be that has only three kinds of synapses? It can be very powerful indeed, as computer science has shown. Everything that a computer does can be handled by different combinations of AND, OR, and NOT gates. The AND gate has two inputs and an output. It passes a signal on if both its inputs carry a signal. The OR gate is similar but passes a signal on if either or both of its inputs are on. The NOT gate simply reverses the signal, turning on when there's no input and turning off when there is.

Each of these has a neurological equivalent. The AND gate corresponds to the synapse that needs input from several places before it fires. The OR gate resembles the synapse that fires if it receives any signal, and the synapse that turns off when it's stimulated is like the NOT gate. With just these three kinds of cells, the nervous system can do everything that the biggest computer can do and much more. On top of that, neurons and synapses grow and die, so brains can and do rewire themselves constantly.[4] And the number of synapses in the human brain is vastly greater than the number of switches in the largest supercomputer yet built.

Such parallels have been enough to set off a chain of guesswork. Because nerve cells are something like the logical gates in a computer, it seems obvious to many people that the brain is nothing but a big computer. And since computers manipulate symbolic information represented as zeros and ones, most people assume that the brain's major business is also the processing of symbols. From here it's easy to draw the final conclusion: that the brain makes symbolic representations of the things that we see or sense outside ourselves and then generates a plan of action accordingly. That's what we see when we imagine our minds at work. If this chain of analogies is true, then, the mind of our conscious experience gives us an accurate picture of what we are in a biological sense.

These assumptions sound very plausible. But remember the caution at the start of this chapter. Two hundred years ago it sounded just as plausible to describe the brain as if it were a mass of clockwork. In reality, the nervous system and the brain itself spend most of their time doing what all other cell signaling systems do: they coordinate other systems. And they don't do this by processing information, which would mean composing and transmitting summaries of the state of those different organs. They do it directly, by transmitting signals that help organs and organisms adjust to one another.

This is not all. There is evidence now that neurons themselves settle into complex resonance patterns by influencing one another outside the firing and dampening of synapses. Other recent research is also showing that the "glial" cells that make up 90 percent of the human brain play a huge and vital role in thinking and acting—and glial cells coordinate through waves of calcium ions, working holistically rather than through structured interactions like computer switches. The central processing unit in the mind isn't as easy to find in the nervous system as you might assume.[5] The more we study the brain, the less it looks like a CPU of a computer.

What's more, in a lot of areas the brain just lets those other systems do all the work. This is just what we'd expect from Darwin's theories. Natural selection favors simple and reliable systems that are highly responsive to the environment, so low-level structures distributed throughout the body and focused on specific tasks are more likely to evolve than centralized, high-level ones that handle many things at once. It's easier for a creature to survive if one of the low-level systems is damaged, and these are also better able to make use of the environment and the physical structure of the animal itself.

A lot of our knowledge is actually outside of us in the world. Imagine, as an analogy, that you need to drive from Boston to Cape Cod after some evil magician has done away with all the roads. You'd need a big off-road vehicle and you'd have a huge number of routes to choose from, and you'd have to find out about the firmness of the soil, how thick the vegetation grows along the way, the location of rivers, and the rise and fall of the land itself. Without that, you'd risk ending up in the mud or facing a cliff.

Deciding on the best route through a roadless wilderness is a huge and probably insoluble task even for a bevy of supercomputers. But you don't have to worry about these problems. There are plenty of good roads between the two places that support the kind of car you're likely to own, and those roads never get too steep or plunge into the water. Choosing a route is a simple matter of looking at a road map (or checking Google) and picking the fast trip by the interstate or the more scenic drive through Plymouth and the cranberry bogs.

In a similar way, much of what we do as biological entities depends on the predictable ways that our bodies respond in predictable environments. That's how insects coordinate the motion of their legs.[6] Moving an insect forward without getting six different legs tangled up with one another is a very complex problem. If the grasshopper or the ant had to work this out in its very tiny brain, it would not have much brain left over—yet it manages this task very well.

Darwin himself was astounded by what seemed to be the exceptional mental powers of such tiny animals. In this instance, though, he was looking in the wrong place. Walking with six legs is a daunting problem in computation, but insects don't even try to go that route. Instead of using their brainpower, they rely on the shape and elasticity of their body parts and the conditions in which they usually walk. Each of their legs has a small cluster of nerves connected with a little stress monitor that "reads" the angle that the leg makes with the trunk. When it reaches a certain angle, the nerves fire and move the leg forward a step.

This works because the insect is almost always walking on a hard and slightly sticky surface. If one leg moves, the position of the whole insect changes. The other feet are still firmly planted, so the other legs swivel where they're joined to the torso. The only information that each leg needs to know is how far it's swiveled. Left leg number two doesn't care about the position of the insect's body or what any of the other legs are doing. It monitors the angle it makes with the body and invariably steps forward just when it should.

Such a system depends on the insect's being the body that it is and its environment staying reasonably constant. It can solve the problem of coordinating six legs under those conditions, just as you can solve the problem of driving to Cape Cod as long as there are roads for you to drive on and a car engineered to travel on those roads. Take those conditions away, and the problem comes back. Turn an insect upside down and its legs flail chaotically. It's as much at a loss as you would be if all the roads in Massachusetts had suddenly disappeared.

There's certainly some signal processing going on here, but on nothing like the scale that would be needed if the problem were left to the brain. A puzzle that is so complex in the abstract is solved by a simple, low-level system that relies on the predictable interactions of the nervous system, the stress sensors in the body, the various different parts of the body of the insect itself, and the world in which the insect finds itself. In this case—and in many others—"thinking" about action is really thinking about the much narrower and more manageable realm of *our* actions in *our* world. That thinking is especially efficient because we and our world evolved together and fit quite closely. For most everyday tasks bottom-up coordination works better than top-down thinking.

Allowing local systems to do some of the work frees the brain up for other jobs, like making sense out of all the stimuli from sense organs, deciding what to do with leftover salmon, and reading books like this one. All the same, there's something a little disturbing about the notion that parts of our body can work more or less on their own. It leaves us feeling as if we're mere passengers in our lives, at the mercy of distributed control systems, and that possibility is no more comforting than the thought that we're just a gene's way of making more genes.

But that's not all. The brain itself is largely terra incognita—an unknown land. Just because something goes on in our brain doesn't mean that it is part of the experience we call having a mind or that we have any control over it. Most of the time we're not even aware of what our brains are up to. Worse yet, when we *do* think that we know what's going on, we're often dead wrong. We assume that our minds are in charge, but it turns out that this confidence isn't scientifically justifiable. The more we find out about ourselves, the more it seems that our minds are just along for the ride. If our brains really were control centers, we wouldn't be whatever it is that controls them.

Some of the first experiments that led in this direction were made by a physiologist named Benjamin Libet in the late 1970s and early 1980s. Libet asked experimental subjects to lift their arm at a time of their choosing, checking their brain waves as they did this. He found unmistakable signs that the subjects' arms began to move before they made any conscious decision to move them.[7] There have been bitter arguments over how these experiments should be interpreted, but Libet's work and more recent, even more rigorous studies have led many researchers to conclude that our conscious "decisions" may be nothing more than a reflection of actions over which we have no conscious control.[8]

This sounds terribly wrong. We can't help but feel that we are independent, self-determined agents who are free to decide on a course of action and carry it out. As other experiments have shown, however, this unshakable sense of personal agency is anything but reliable. As psychologist Daniel Wegner explains in his book *The Illusion of Conscious Will*, we have separate neurological processes to generate actions and to ascribe intentions and "claim" acts as our own.[9] There's no direct connection between these two, no internal signal that tells the brain, "This is something that I decided to do." Instead, we nurse a number of subconscious ideas about what we want, and whenever we see ourselves doing something that fits one of those ideas, we assume that the action is intentional. It makes no difference if we caused them or not; actions seem willed whenever they coincide with our subconscious intentions. Like a cartoon character, we catch ourselves in the act and immediately shout, "I meant to do that!"

This arrangement works fairly well, but it also leads us to make up reasons for actions that we clearly didn't originate. Wegner quotes this passage from a nineteenth-century expert in hypnotism, Albert Moll:

> I tell a hypnotized subject that when he wakes he is to take a flower-pot from the window, wrap it in a cloth, put it on the sofa, and bow to it three times. All which he does. When he is asked for his reasons he answers, "You know, when I woke and saw the flower-pot there I thought that as it was rather cold the flower-pot had better be warmed a little, or else the plant would die. So I wrapped it in the cloth, and then I thought that as the sofa was near the fire I would put the flower-pot on it; and I bowed because I was pleased with myself for having such a bright idea." He added that he did not

consider the proceeding foolish, he had told me his reasons for so acting. In this case the subject carried out an absurd post-hypnotic suggestion; he was unconscious of the constraint put upon him and
tried to find good reasons for his act. Most experimenters have
observed that their subjects try to find reasons for the most foolish
suggested acts.[10]

The hypnotic subject didn't remember the suggestion, of course, so
he couldn't blame his actions on the hypnotist. But he could not tolerate the possibility that he acted with no reason at all. This thought
would be too great a threat to his confidence that he was in control of
himself. The only way out of that bind was for him to come up with
a good reason for every one of his meaningless acts.

Wegner suggests that we would rather invent such absurd explanations for our actions than admit that we act unconsciously. Moll's
plant-loving subject wasn't exactly lying. He believed what he said,
thereby preserving his self-image as what Wegner calls an "ideal
agent" who does what he wants to do and never does anything else.
If he was lying, he was lying to himself first of all.

The technical term for such self-deception is confabulation, and
some of the most astonishing examples of confabulation come from
people with brain damage. The neurologist V. S. Ramachandran
relates a conversation with one stroke patient:

> Mrs. Dodds knew what had happened and was aware of her
> surroundings.
> "Okay," I said. "And how are you feeling now?"
> "Fine."
> "Can you walk?"
> "Sure I can walk." Mrs. Dodds had been lying in her bed or sitting
> propped up in a wheelchair for the past two weeks. She had not taken
> a single step since her fall in the bathroom.
> "What about your hands? Hold out your hands. Can you move
> them?"
> Mrs. Dodds seemed mildly annoyed at the question. "Of course I can
> use my hands." . . .

"Can you touch my nose with your left hand?"
Her hands lay paralyzed in front of her.
"Mrs. Dodds, are you touching my nose?"
"Yes, of course I'm touching your nose."
"Can you actually see yourself touching my nose?"
"Yes, I can see it. It's less than an inch from your face."[11]

Patients like Mrs. Dodds suffer from anosognosia, a complete failure to realize that they're sick. Her claims to do things that she clearly couldn't do shows how strong the compulsion is to claim ownership of any action that coincides with our intentions. We act and imagine that we must have chosen to act that way—taking the deed for the wish, if you like. Mrs. Dodd's stroke had upset this arrangement by cutting off her knowledge of her physical acts. She was no longer aware of what her body was doing, so she didn't know that she *hadn't* moved her arm. The processes that ascribe intentions now spun their wheels in a vacuum, imagining actions simply because the intentions were present—taking the wish for the deed.

For the rest of us, of course, feedback from muscles and our other senses keeps us from claiming acts that didn't happen in the first place. But as Wegner's and Libet's research suggests, we can't take our own sense of agency at face value, either. We confabulate in just the same way that Mrs. Dodds did, the big difference being that an undamaged nervous system offers up only real physical actions for our approval and the stamp of intention. We certainly do act with deliberation and intention, but this doesn't happen the way we think it does, and it isn't as consistent as we imagine it to be. The hard truth is that our claim to will the real things that we do is almost as untrustworthy as her claim to will the things that she didn't.

There's a consistent picture emerging from this and other work in neurology and psychology. We're learning the following:

- Our reasons for actions generally come after the fact, just like our claim to have intended them.

- We can set and pursue goals without any conscious awareness.[12]
- Devoting conscious thought to a complex problem leads to poor solutions compared with putting the problem aside and concentrating on something else.[13]
- Our choices are motivated mainly by emotions, not reason.[14]
- We can't make purely rational decisions anyway because without emotion leading the way, our decisions are rarely appropriate.[15]
- Those emotions are shaped by events in and around our body as a whole.[16]
- The nerves in our intestines—the enteric nervous system—influence our mood, emotional state, and action more than anyone had suspected.[17]
- In general, conscious thinking is "a limited capacity system used for problem solving superimposed on a set of competing, collaborating, and conflicting unconscious processes."[18] We are creatures of emotion and unconscious impulse.

It looks very much as if he subjective mind is nothing but a mode of experience, a misleading one at that, little more than a pretty picture show. The power that we think we have to rise above our biological urges and primitive feelings, choose rational goals, and live a life according to reason—the aim of philosophy since Socrates at least—looks more and more like a pathetic delusion.

From an evolutionary perspective none of this should be a surprise. The self-conscious mind looks like it's in charge, and our actions seem to be wholly under our conscious control. But most if not all other animals do without one; they manage their affairs quite well through unconscious processes. Natural selection is not likely to have led to a completely different action and perception system for our species alone. It's much more probable that self-consciousness evolved as a few tweaks on a set of systems that had been tried and tested in cats, bat, rats, and every other kind of living thing. (This is what Darwin thought.) It's almost certainly nothing like what it appears to be.

These are disturbing results. It doesn't seem much better to be run by an organic, responsive body than it does to be run by a mechanical, clockwork body and its internal genetic program. But there's one question that we haven't answered. If our actions aren't programmed by genes and if they're not the commands of a sovereign mind, where do they come from?

The answer is simple but profound in its implications. In the previous chapter, we talked about the importance of coordination. We saw that our cells are constantly responding to one another, weaving an unhierarchical web of influences through which they all work together without any direction from outside. This kind of interactivity doesn't stop at the cellular level. Other, even more extraordinary research is showing that some of our nervous system evolved for the very same kind of coordination.

Our bodies have minds of their own, but they're not isolated, individual minds. They're parts of a much wider community, woven more intimately than the closest embrace. We're aligned with other people's actions and emotions through the ebb and flow of our feelings and through coordinated activity. We knit the same kind of free, unhierarchical network with one another that we saw inside our own bodies. In our self-conscious thoughts we are all isolated individuals, but we, our neighbors, and our world are one in our bodies and our actions. Our emotions and decisions come from everyone and everywhere. We feel and act together. *All the living world plays its part in the life of the body.*

This is where agency and freedom become real. We are not puppets. Ideal agency is an illusion, but the mistake behind it isn't the belief that we make our world. It lies in the belief that each one of us makes her *own* world. Our agency is genuine, but we act and will as part of the totality of beings—never in isolation. We share control of and responsibility for the entire world. Acting with and for all others, we have real agency, and because there is nothing outside the give-and-take of that shared agency, we have real freedom, too.

This is an extraordinary claim, but the evidence supporting it is all around us. It starts from things we've always noticed. Researchers in child development as well as doting parents have watched newborns coordinating movement with their mothers only 18 hours after birth. Even in adults, emotions and actions like yawning are often contagious. People living in close relations tend to imitate one another unconsciously, a phenomenon sometimes called the "chameleon effect." Members of different communities share patterns of thought, feeling, and experience, and these go beyond anything that we would expect from a common language or conscious instruction.

We are clearly connected with one another in all kinds of ways, and we are attuned to one another more deeply than we usually recognize. Yet it was not until 1995 that a clearer picture began to emerge of the full range and scope of our interconnection. In that year, Vittorio Gallese, Giacomo Rizzolatti, and other neurologists at the University of Parma in Italy discovered some unusual nerve cells in the brains of macaque monkeys. They were motor neurons, the kind that fire to direct actions, and like other motor neurons, they activated when the monkeys performed a specific action, such as grasping a piece of food. But they also fired when the monkey was merely observing someone else—monkey or human—performing the same action. Because the neurons in the observer mirrored the neurons in the active monkey, the scientists dubbed them "mirror neurons."[19]

This was only the first of a cascade of astonishing discoveries. Mirror neurons have been found in all primates, including humans. Some echo actions that are only partially seen, and others mirror actions that are only heard. Experiments have shown that certain mirror neurons fire when an action is directed at a specific result. They might activate only when the context suggests eating, for instance, and remain dormant when the context is neutral or suggests something less interesting, such as cleaning up.

Thanks to yet other mirror neurons, we ourselves feel the touch of a hand on someone else's skin and experience their emotional states and pain. There are neurons that activate when we smile and when we see someone smile, when we experience disgust and see someone visibly disgusted, and so on—one reason that moods can be so contagious.

Through such selective responses, we are immediately changed by the intentions of others as well as by their acts. The life of those around us is reflected within ourselves. Not all motor neurons are mirror neurons, of course, and for this and other reasons, those acts and feelings don't live in us in their full color and depth. But they help us connect with and coordinate with others directly and wordlessly. There is no need for overt interpretation or for any conscious thinking at all.

Actions aren't "owned" by the actor alone, and we don't keep our feelings and intentions inside. All these move through the world like the wind, transforming each individual who breathes them in and out and picking up those people's feelings, actions, and desires and carrying those forward, too. This back-and-forth feedback between apparently separate and isolated individuals works much like the back-and-forth flow of signals inside each of our bodies. In the same way that individual cells coordinate their activity, we harmonize our activities through what Gallese has called "intentional attunement."[20]

Our bodies prompt us to act, and we sense our bodily states as emotions, but those are not our promptings alone, and the emotions are not private, either. These come not just from our own individual body but from many others as well. Since we know and are changed by everyone around us, our own acts are theirs, too. Since others are affected by our acts and feelings, we act through them as they act through us. Agency is real, but it is fundamentally plural.

Here, then, is another and entirely unexpected function for the nervous system. The mirror neurons in the brain act as a kind of sixth sense (or seventh if we count proprioception, the sense of the body's state and position). Their "output" affects only the body, so we are rarely aware of what we know this way, but through it our bodies, at least, comprehend and echo the lives of those around us. If the nervous system is something like a wired network, the flow of feelings, intentions, and actions through the activity of mirror neurons can be compared to a wireless one. It is the most surprising of the many networks of coordination that underpin all life: systems of chemical signals, specialized chemical messages sent through the bloodstream, the high-speed wiring of the nervous system, and the "WiFi" of mirror neurons that sets us to resonate with those around us.

As religious sages have always told us, we are not at all the way we appear to ourselves. The commonsense view is that we're separate and isolated beings. We identify with our thoughts, and we are alone with them, too. Even if a friend sincerely wants to know how we feel, it is a struggle to explain ourselves in a way that she can understand without coming out with a dumbed-down betrayal of our real feelings. Yet silence can do this job better than language. In rare moments, words will fall dead, we let ourselves reflect each other, and suddenly there seems to be no problem at all. In the luminous intensity of that connection, we simply *know* each other to the core. In such encounters, the real character of our lives opens up to us. We live in and through one another, so woven together that we cannot be untangled.

Mirror neurons connect us with other people, but they do not appear to respond to the actions of nonhuman animals.[21] Our embraidedness doesn't stop at the line between human and nonhuman beings, though. Anyone who lives closely with a pet or with livestock feels certain that they respond to our emotions and actions and that we respond to theirs. There's no reason to dismiss this. These ties come out of a more basic, nonneurological connection, the structural coupling, briefly mentioned in the previous chapter, through which all life is woven together. In this respect, we're a lot like dogs, cats, or sheep. We sense emotions from posture, movement, and facial expressions; so do they. Mirror neurons work so well because they build on these other layers of bodily coordination, exactly as we rely on the physical qualities of our bodies and the stable features of our world when we walk or jump.

Scientists in several fields are beginning to talk of "distributed cognition," a kind of thinking that goes on among individuals instead of inside them. As primatologists Louise Barrett and Peter Henzi have written,

> Cognition is not limited by the "skin and skull" of the individual, but uses resources and materials in the environment [like the insect's use of the properties of its legs]. The dynamic social interaction of primates are thus "not pointers to a private cognition" but can be investigated as cognitive processes in themselves. A distributed approach . . . considers all cognitive processes to emerge from the interactions between individuals, and between individuals and the world.[22]

We rely on distributed cognition for most of what makes life possible and almost all of what makes it sweet. Emotional know-how and empathy depend on it, and many researchers suspect that autism and other disorders of empathy are caused by problems with the mirror neuron system and perhaps other forms of emotional coordination.[23]

But we also count on mirror neurons when we learn new skills. A child finds out how to rewire a light switch as she watches her father, and those gestures become part of her body long before she dares to act on her embodied knowledge. A satisfactory conversation happens when the participants simply open themselves to one another and leave off drafting responses as they listen. A good trial lawyer knows when she should throw out her written summation and tell the jury something else. She knows in her bones when they're siding with her client and when they aren't. Where your opponent is likely to direct the next serve, which candidate is likely to start a war if elected, who you should choose to confess your deepest secrets to—knowing these things isn't a matter of applying a correct theory to carefully observed data. It comes from the thoughts and feelings that pass among people and between people and their world.

The conventional wisdom is that these insights come from a "theory of mind," a special brain module through which we analyze and anticipate other people's intentions. Dennett, who has been one of the foremost proponents of a theory-based theory of mind, thinks of people along the lines of the detective in a crime novel.[24] According to him, we make our way through the social world by keeping a close eye on those around us, picking up and assembling clues, and consulting our internal theory-of-mind handbook to decide what everyone's likely to do next.

Since we have immediate, bodily knowledge of what other people intend, do, and feel, though, we don't need to flip through *The Junior Woodchuck's Guide to Understanding Other People* or such in a department of the brain. We know roughly what other people intend because we experience their intentions directly. Ordinary intelligence can take care of the details. And though we don't actually read off the results, these become conscious in our intuitive awareness that a new employee is up to no good, that our wife is planning a surprise birthday party, that our son wants to eat another cookie, or that the girl who I wanted to ask to the prom is about to throw her arms around my best friend and kiss him.

In evolutionary terms, mirror neurons are far more likely a development than a theory-of-mind module. They build on existing forms of coordination and "repurpose" existing cells to exploit their existing properties for different ends. This has happened over and over in evolutionary history, and the trick of using a motor system for interpersonal coordination as well would not be unusual. The evolution of Dennett's theory-of-mind module, like the all-powerful conscious mind of our commonsense ideas, would be something that happens rarely if it has happened at all: the appearance of a dedicated, single-function system using completely new "technology" that takes over from another, older system.

Of course, Dennett's theory doesn't shake our deep-seated belief that we're the masters of our fate and rulers of the private kingdom of the mind. That's why it sounds plausible to many people. The view we've developed here is more unnerving, but admitting that our commonsense image is a delusion and that we depend on the body's knowledge seems far less frightening once we think in terms of distributed cognition. Conscious thoughts are private, but through the body we think publicly—and we think better that way because we know more. Since the body is open and the conscious mind is not, acting on our emotions is not the same as ignoring reality and surrendering to misguided or selfish urges. It's the only way we can align ourselves with the knowledge that flows through the body, and it's the best way to live for others as well as for ourselves.

Mirror neurons also explain one of the profoundest mysteries of human life. All people, everywhere and in every time, seem to share fundamental ideas of right and wrong, and in spite of reasons to do the opposite, most people try to be good to others. People will sacrifice their own interests and sometimes even their own lives for what they believe is the greater good and for perfect strangers. We're lucky that this is so because life would be pretty hard if it weren't. Yet theories like Dawkins's can't account for altruism or morality. In Dawkins's view, these are either strategies for spreading our relatives' genes or "blessed misfirings" of other, equally selfish behaviors.[25]

So where does morality come from? Thinkers like Marc Hauser have argued that our ideas of right and wrong are encoded in yet another high-tech mind module, this time a morality module.[26] But mirror neurons provide a better explanation. Morality is a bottom-up phenomenon. It comes from the way we feel when we are truly open to one another and when life flows freely between us.

This doesn't happen often. At rare and precious moments, though, we find ourselves fully open to that flow of feeling and action. I have no sense that I'm being asked to conform to your intentions, and you don't need to bend to meet mine. Nothing checks what passes between us. What I do finds an immediate echo in you, and your response meshes perfectly with mine. We let go of our private interests and goals and live in and through the give-and-take of emotion as easily as breathing in and out. The taste of such moments is unique. When two, three, or a whole room of people are so enmeshed, we feel elated, calm, and free. Everything goes effortlessly, exactly as everything needs to.

Surprisingly, this is what we might expect from the way mirror neurons work. At any given moment, the mirror neurons in your brain will take a backseat to your emotions and your intentions. Other people's emotions and intentions are present, but they're not as strong. If what you do finds an echo in others, though, their intentions begin to line up with yours. You sense this change in the new state of your nervous system because some of the same neurons now fire for other people's emotions and intentions as well as your own. The tracings of everyone's feelings and intentions begins to coincide, and you and your friends subtly shift your precise intentions to the joint intention that begins to emerge.

Everyone who acts on this concurrence carries other peoples' intentions forward with their own. The harmony among you grows, and everyone's interactions become more and more effortless. Your actual neurological states are coordinated, not because you've all committed to a specific project or submitted to some higher authority but because each of you has opened to the intentions of the others. The common project emerges from that interplay as if it had a life of its own, and nobody is in charge except the group itself.

Although the mirror neuron system probably doesn't account for all of this, it's certainly a factor. It links us loosely together in a kind of neural net, a web connecting many nodes that's not unlike a complicated version of the hydra's nervous system. It's been known for decades that all such neural networks tend to settle into states where each signal source reinforces the others, producing exactly the kind of harmony we've been talking about.

Such times of ease, mutual acceptance, and connection serve as touchstones for ethical behavior. Our deep sense of the good grows from there, through memories that go back to the bond between mother and child, the "primary intersubjectivity" that comes even before mirror neurons develop in the infant's brain.[27] (One famous if much-criticized study claimed that the one phrase that evokes the greatest positive response when flashed subliminally is "mommy and I are one."[28]) We are rooted in one another, and we feel fully human only when we breathe and act together. Mirror neurons help us open to that state, and when their influence is combined with other kinds of intersubjective coordination, they make for some of the richest experiences in life.

Perfect ease like this demands only one simple but hard thing: that we let go of our own ideas and our own demands. The first and foremost ethical experience is one of selflessness—of surrendering the isolated stance of the mind and accepting the openness of the body. Only then, having lost ourselves, do we find that we and the world are one.

This bodily experience is surely the root of the spiritual unity that every religion seeks. He who would save his life must lose it, said Jesus; judge not, lest ye be judged. A popular American minister reminds us that "this is not about you." Zen Buddhists are told that every day is a beautiful day, and the Hebrew Bible blesses the day that the Lord has made—and of course, he has made all of them, the ones we find terrible along with the ones we find good. It is for this reason that Muslims shout "God is great" in moments of terrible loss and Jews gather at gravesides to read a prayer that contains nothing but praise of God. These are the moments when we are most tempted to armor ourselves and reject the ebb and flow of life itself, when we want one feeling to cancel out all the others, and when we want to kick God off the throne and take over. Nothing keeps us from doing this, but it is always a Pyrrhic victory. To deny death and suffering is to die to life.

In ordinary times, at least, we know enough of the bliss and peace of selflessness that we are drawn to it. Virtue really is its own reward.

No morality module or code of ethics is required; bodily knowledge is enough. Through our own body, open to all others, we are best placed to satisfy the rules laid down by the greatest of Western ethical philosophers, Immanuel Kant. We can act, simply and gracefully, as we would hope that everyone would act: to give effect to the feelings and intentions of everyone, ourselves included. We treat every person as an end and not just as a means—one version of Kant's famous "categorical imperative"—because every person is given a voice in our actions. What we want could be universal law—another version of the imperative—and in fact it is universal law because our embraidedness finds the points of true harmony among our friends and neighbors and their friends and neighbors and so on. We may forget Kant's words and his formulations, but through the knowledge of the body we can live their spirit, which is the real "moral law."

But what about the times when a sense of what's right leads a person to stand up against others, perhaps even the whole community? Shouldn't the flow of mirrored emotion simply force us to become sheeplike conformists? There's no reason that it should. We ourselves are as much a participant in this silent conversation as anyone else. We bring to it our memories and our own touchstones for genuinely connected, fully ethical life, and we guide ourselves by the memory of what it feels like to be fully human. We know in our hearts that some kinds of unity are forced and one-sided, and we know, too, when we are asked to ignore the pain of wronging someone else. Moral strength comes from the deeper knowledge of the body, which is far more reliable than the endless word spinning of the mind. Only the body can tell us whether we are surrounded by the blessed community or the living dead. The mind gets too often fooled.

It is not reason but emotion that tells us what we must not do, that warns us that some acts will poison our lives so deeply that we will never be at peace with ourselves again. One of the most terrifying documents to come from the Holocaust is a 1943 speech by Heinrich Himmler to a group of SS men praising their heroism in stifling their fellow feeling for Jews to do the work that logic told them to do. We might pause here to think about this. The SS men knew that they were doing something terrible, but they deliberately suppressed their revulsion because they had convinced themselves that they were doing something necessary. In that case, at least, the body was far more moral than the mind.

Mirror neurons are a new discovery, but the flow of feeling and knowledge they make possible has been discovered in many cultures and goes by many names. It is surely what leads toward the ultimate unity of all things that Hindus call brahman and the all-embracing this-worldly connection that the Chinese call Tao. German philosophers of the 1790s and early 1800s took it as the inner movement of reason, which for them meant a community's spontaneous creation of new forms of understanding and new ways of life.

As all these traditions tell us, this luminous, living harmony is our real home and our real nature. In it, we are profoundly united with one another and profoundly free. But there's just one problem with this. *Life almost never feels that way.*

Notes

1. Anne O'Daley, ed., *Encyclopedia of life sciences*, vol. 2 (New York: Marshall Cavendish, 2004), 258.
2. This is something of an oversimplification because there is some evidence that the hydra's net of nerves is polarized and can convey the location of the stimulus. It is uncertain, though, how much the hydra makes use of this. See H. Shimizu, "Feeding and wounding responses in *Hydra* suggest functional and structural polarization of the tentacle nervous system," *Comparative Biochemistry and Physiology, Part A* 131 (2002): 669–74. The polarization of primitive nerve nets is a matter of controversy, however; see C. R. Gallistel, *The organization of action: A new synthesis* (Hillsdale, NJ: Lawrence Erlbaum Associates, 1980), 46.

3. See, for example, O. Koizumi, "Nerve ring of the hypostome in hydra: Is it an origin of the central nervous system of bilaterian animals?," *Brain, Behavior and Evolution* 69, no. 2 (2007): 151–59.

4. This happens most of all in young children, which is why they learn so rapidly, but it continues at a slower pace throughout life.

5. A semipopular account is Andrew Koob, *The root of thought: Unlocking glia—The brain cell that will help us sharpen our wits, heal injury, and treat brain disease* (Upper Saddle River, NJ: FT Press, 2009).

6. This example draws from Rolf Pfeifer and Josh Bongard, *How the body shapes the way we think: A new view of intelligence* (Cambridge, MA: MIT Press, 2007).

7. The most convenient summary of his work is in his book for general readers; see Benjamin Libet, *Mind-time: The temporal factor in consciousness* (Cambridge, MA: Harvard University Press, 2004); his attempt at reserving a space for free will seems to me unconvincing, however.

8. C. S. Soon, M. Brass, H.-J. Heinze, and J.-D. Haynes, "Unconscious determinants of free decisions in the human brain," *Nature Neuroscience* 11 (2008): 543–45. See, generally, Kerri Smith, "Neuroscience vs philosophy: Taking aim at free will," *Nature* 477 (2011): 23–25, doi:10.1038/477023a.

9. Daniel Wegner, *The illusion of conscious will* (Cambridge, MA: MIT Press, 2002).

10. Wegner, *The illusion of conscious will*, 150.

11. V. S. Ramachandran and Sandra Blakeslee, *Phantoms in the brain: Probing the mysteries of the human mind* (New York: Morrow, 1998), 128–29.

12. See John A. Bargh, "What have we been priming all these years? On the development, mechanisms, and ecology of nonconscious social behavior," *European Journal of Social Psychology* 36 (2006): 147–68; John A. Bargh, and Melissa J. Ferguson, "Beyond behaviorism: On the automaticity of higher mental processes," *Psychological Bulletin* 126, no. 6 (2000): 925–45; and John A. Bargh, and Tanya L. Chartrand, "The unbearable automaticity of being," *American Psychologist* 54, no. 7 (1999): 462–79.

13. M. W. Bos, A. Dijksterhuis, and R. B. van Baaren, "On the goal-dependency of unconscious thought," *Journal of Experimental Social Psychology* 44 (2008): 1114–20; Ap Dijksterhuis et al., "On making the right choice: The deliberation-without-attention effect," *Science*

311 (2006): 1005; A. Dijksterhuis and L. F. Nordgren, "A theory of unconscious thought," *Perspectives on Psychological Science* 1 (2006): 95–109.

14. This is the theme of Antonio Damasio, *Descartes' error: Emotion, reason and the human brain* (New York: Vintage, 2006).

15. See, for example, the well-known story of Phineas Gage, whose contact with emotion was destroyed in a railroad accident; Damasio, *Descartes' error*, 3–51.

16. See, generally, Jordan Zlatev, ed., *The shared mind: Perspectives on intersubjectivity* (Amersterdam: John Benjamins, 2008); Hanne De Jaegher, Ezequiel Di Paolo, and Shaun Gallagher, "Can social interaction constitute social cognition?," *Trends in Cognitive Science* 14, no. 10 (2010): 441–47; papers of Shaun Gallagher linked at http://pegasus.cc.ucf.edu/~gallaghr/gallonline.html; Hanne De Jaegher, "Social understanding through direct perception? Yes, by interacting," *Consciousness and Cognition* 18 (2009): 535–42; and Thomas Fuchs and Hanne De Jaegher, "Enactive intersubjectivity: Participatory sense-making and mutual incorporation," *Phenomenology and the Cognitive Sciences* 8 (2009): 465–86.

17. K. Neufeld et al., "Reduced anxiety-like behavior and central neurochemical change in germ-free mice," *Neurogastroenterology and Motility* 23 (2011), http://scienceblogs.com/neurophilosophy/2011/03/gut_bacteria_may_influence_thoughts_and_behaviour.php.

18. Drew Westen, Joel Weinberger, and Rebekah Bradley, "Motivation, decision making, and consciousness: From psychodynamics to subliminal priming and emotional constraint satisfaction," in *The Cambridge handbook of consciousness*, ed. Philip David Zelazo, Morris Moscovitch, and Evan Thompson (Cambridge: Cambridge University Press, 2007), 673.

19. A popular presentation of this research is found in Marco Iacoboni, *Mirroring people: The new science of how we connect with others* (New York: Macmillan, 2008), but more provocative are the papers of Gallese, in particular, available online at http://www.unipr.it/arpa/mirror/english/staff/gallese.htm.

20. By this, he meant the way our intentions harmonize, not that we go about doing this intentionally.

21. This is the answer to the zombie problem, by the way; we know that other people are people like us because we feel their experience in a unique way.

22. Louise Barrett and Peter Henzi, "The social nature of primate cognition," *Proceedings of the Royal Society B* 272 (2005): 1869.
23. V. S. Ramachandran, *The tell-tale brain: A neuroscientist's quest for what makes us human* (New York: Norton, 2011), 136.
24. There are competing schools of thought on theory of mind. Those who think we concoct ideas about others' acts and intentions espouse theory-theory of mind, and those who think we run internal models of others argue for simulation theory of mind.
25. Richard Dawkins, *The God delusion* (New York: Houghton Mifflin Harcourt, 2008), 252, 254.
26. Marc Hauser, *Moral minds: How nature designed our universal sense of right and wrong* (New York: HarperCollins, 2006).
27. Colin Trevarthen, "Communication and cooperation in early infancy: A description of primary intersubjectivity," in *Before speech: The beginning of interpersonal communication*, ed. Margaret Bullowa (Cambridge: CUP Archive, 1979), 321–48.
28. Lloyd H. Silverman and Joel Weinberger, "Mommy and I are one: Implications for psychotherapy," *American Psychologist* 40 (1985): 1296–308.

6

Self-Awareness Is a Very Dangerous Gift

What we've found our way to is a very old difficulty, usually called the problem of evil. It's not a surprise that the monotheisms face it; they teach that the universe was set up by an all-knowing being who has the power to create anything he chooses, who continues to determine everything that happens, and who loves his creation with infinite love. Where, then, could evil come from? How could an omnipotent, omniscient, and loving god stand by and let terrible things happen? Why did he set up the universe so terrible things could happen in the first place? Some theologians tell us that there are deep reasons for giving us the freedom that lets us murder, maim, neglect, or oppress others. Even if we accept this as a reasonable explanation of specifically human ills, though, it still wouldn't explain why the creator designed a world with tornadoes, malaria, heart attacks, AIDS, tsunamis, brain tumors that grow in infants, and the wasting diseases of age.

Evil isn't just a problem for the monotheisms, however. Getting rid of the idea of a transcendental creator means that we don't have to explain away death, disease, and natural disasters, but that still leaves a lot of questions unanswered. The world is far sadder than it has to be, and people are far more cruel. Think of the everyday oppression of others by our social and economic arrangements, our countless wars, the random violence in most every city of the world, sexual exploitation, emotional blackmail, the unmotivated nastiness that we usually shrug off, and the barely felt but real coldness that poisons almost every life, no matter how enlightened, comfortable, or monied; how did all this come about? If we really are seamlessly interwoven with all others, why do we ignore, manipulate, or oppress them? Why are we as a species so violent? What makes war such a fixed part of human history in spite of the fact that almost everyone claims to hate it? What makes us mean, and what makes us so bad?

One fashionable and scientific-sounding explanation, "social Darwinism," asserts that evolution rewards the ruthless. Cruelty and exploitation are in our genes, viciousness is innate, and there's nothing we can do about it and nothing to apologize for. That's why social Darwinism is fashionable in times of runaway greed and unregulated capitalism, especially among the greedy and the rich who trumpet it as proof that they deserve their wealth. A hundred years ago, when John D. Rockefeller's Standard Oil Trust controlled more than 90 percent of American oil production, the tycoon modestly explained his success with these words: "The growth of a large business is merely a survival of the fittest. . . . The American Beauty rose can be produced in the splendor and fragrance which bring cheer to its beholder only by sacrificing the early buds which grow up around it."

But social Darwinism is bad science and has almost nothing in common with Darwin's real theory. Natural selection doesn't operate on cultural groups or business organizations. Neither does it select for aggression or a talent for conquest. Fitness in evolutionary terms means the ability to thrive and reproduce in the environmental niche where the organism finds itself, not the strength to grow bigger than anyone else. Ruthlessness is not favored unless it can reliably lead to the survival of more descendants. It rarely does.

Back in the nineteenth century, the colonial powers in Europe often claimed that their military victories justified their rule over "inferior races"; if Indians and Africans weren't inferior, the logic ran, they wouldn't have lost. It's true that if two populations compete for the same resources, a particularly aggressive group might kill or drive out the other. But this wouldn't really be a test of fitness. A population that's successful at conquest may be a sorry failure at long-term survival. It may run through the resources of its new home in a few generations and die out. If it had exterminated a species with a more sustainable relationship with its surroundings, we'd have to say that the victors turned out to be less fit than the population they replaced.[1]

This is probably why there is little in the natural world that can be compared with human aggressiveness. Herbivores tend to spend their day finding and eating lots of plants and avoiding being eaten by other animals. There's no room for advancement. The John D. Rockefeller of cows might keep lesser cows out of her pasture, but she couldn't eat any more grass than she did before. Her male counterpart might cover a larger number of cows than other bulls and might even fight other bulls for the honor, but there's a natural limit to the number of cows that any bull can mate with and manage.

Carnivores are not that different. Their aggressive defense of territory is anything but competitive. It's more like a lawyers' settlement conference where everyone blusters until a compromise is worked out. To survive as a hunter—whether you're a wolf, a cougar, or a human—you need a hunting territory of your own. Carnivores' mutual aggression results in a balance of power; it carves up the countryside into well-defined hunting grounds, each the right size to support its hunter. As long as populations are steady, it generally produces an equitable division of the land and a stable set of relationships.

A hunter's territory can't shrink below a certain size, and poachers can't be allowed to kill too many of the animals there. If either of these happens, all the hunting skills in the world won't yield enough meat to keep the hunter's family alive. But there's no reason to claim anything more than a reliable subsistence. Staking out too large of a hunting ground is foolish and self-defeating. Hunting is hard work, and patrolling and defending more land than you need is a waste of time and energy. No intelligent hunter will exhaust him- or herself protecting a personal empire if the family could eat just as well from a smaller territory. The only efficient strategy is to claim no more land than you need to survive in leaner years, and that's the strategy that natural selection rewards.

We can't ignore cases of offensive aggression, but these almost always involve a young animal looking for a hunting ground of her own or competition for diminishing resources as environments change. These struggles are more bitter, and losing them is more disastrous, but they still don't resemble the destructive competitiveness of social Darwinist ideology.

There is one natural situation where constant competition *is* fostered, however. Many animals, like chickens, English badgers, and most great apes, live in hierarchical groups.[2] Status usually determines who has access to the more desirable mates, and high-status individuals also get more food. In such groups, every individual is always fighting to keep his or her position.

Hierarchical societies of any sort are often unpleasant and nasty, and we might wonder how this arrangement benefits anyone but the alpha male. The most likely answer is that hierarchies serve to coordinate the group as a whole. There's strength in numbers. There are clear evolutionary advantages to both herding and hunting in packs, and hierarchies are useful—thought not the only—ways of keeping such groups organized.

We humans, like the other apes, come with a strong competitive drive. What's more, most of us have been living in hierarchical groups for thousands of years, since the rise of agricultural civilization. Is this a promising place to look for the roots of evil? Are the social Darwinists right? Are we hierarchical animals and really can't do anything about it?

This sounds like a plausible explanation, but it falls apart once we look at human history in a longer perspective. We *used* to do something about it, and we did it very successfully, too. The age of civilization is only a small part of the human story. For most of our past we lived in egalitarian communities where men and women were roughly equal, where decisions were made by consensus, and where concentrations of power were resisted, sometimes by force. Life was not free from competitiveness or violence, of course, but the basic equality of wealth and power in such groups kept them from growing into aggression and oppression.

This is the crucial distinction between human hunting bands and those of most other apes. Our more complex, balanced, and nuanced kind of social organization probably owed a lot to our capacity for language, which gave us an alternative to hierarchy as a form of group coordination. We could talk things over instead of jockeying for position and following the leader, and this made it possible to trump a biological history of hierarchy with a culture of equality and mutuality.[3]

Anthropologist Christopher Boehm has argued that human prehistory began with an "egalitarian revolution" that broke with our hierarchical past.[4] But this revolution ultimately failed. A counterrevolution of hierarchy and oppression came back at the dawn of civilization with a brutality and nastiness that was much worse than anything seen in other animals. We have lived with that ever since.

So we're still faced with the problem of evil and the question of its origins. What is it in human beings that undermined the egalitarian revolution? What survived in us and subverted the practices that hunting people relied on to limit personal power?

Let us look, for a moment, at the details of one traditional explanation, the story of Adam and Eve.[5] You might remember that there are two forbidden trees in the Garden of Eden, not one. The first tree is the Tree of Life, and eating its fruit makes you immortal. The other is the Tree of the Knowledge of Good and Evil, and that's the one that gets our ancestors into trouble.

It was a very odd kind of trouble, however. As soon as Adam and Eve ate its fruit, "the eyes of them both were opened, and they knew that they were naked; and they sewed fig leaves together, and made themselves aprons." Then, "in the cool of the day," the couple "heard the voice of the LORD God walking in the garden and . . . they hid themselves . . . amongst the trees." God calls out to his creation, and Adam explains, "I heard thy voice in the garden, and I was afraid, because I was naked; and I hid myself."

God then asks, "Who told thee that thou wast naked?"[6]

This is a strange and unexpected question, and it's the most illuminating moment in the entire story of the Fall. If eating the forbidden fruit had imparted nothing more than a knowledge of good and evil, our ancestors' sin would have been the acquisition of a code of morals. Not only would this make no sense as a kind of sin, it would have led God to ask something like, "How didst thou know that nakedness was unseemly?" Something else must have happened when Adam and Eve ate the fruit. The Bible tells us what that was; as we read just above, their *"eyes . . . were opened; and they knew that they were naked."*

In other words, at the moment that they ate the fatal fruit Adam and Eve became self-conscious beings. They woke from a dreamlike state and became like us—acutely, painfully aware of themselves. And in that same moment they found themselves separated from God. As God's question shows us, the knowledge that cost us our innocence was the ability to see ourselves from the outside. Thinking that nakedness is wrong is one thing. Being able to see that you yourself are naked is quite another, and it's this knowledge that's at the heart of Adam's sin.

That is one deep truth of the story of the Fall. The root of our exceptional capacity for evil is the deeply ambiguous gift of self-consciousness, which comes at a terrible price: a disconnection from the interwoven fabric of reality.[7] No other animal appears to share this. To understand the uniqueness of human conduct, then, we need to look at the uniqueness of the human animal, and that means understanding how self-consciousness works and why natural selection might have favored it.

We can't say for certain what led to the evolution of self-consciousness, but Darwin sketched one likely explanation in a few passages in *The Descent of Man*. Darwin's wasn't a finished theory. It can stand some revisions, and it doesn't explain everything, but it gives us some rich and fruitful hints of what self-consciousness is for.

Darwin started his account with a strange and sad phenomenon found among migratory birds:

> Every one knows how strong the maternal instinct is, leading even timid birds to face great danger, though with hesitation, and in opposition to the instinct of self-preservation. Nevertheless, the migratory instinct is so powerful, that late in the autumn swallows, house-martins, and swifts frequently desert their tender young, leaving them to perish miserably in their nests. . . . At the proper season these birds seem all day long to be impressed with the desire to migrate; their habits change; they become restless, are noisy and congregate in flocks. Whilst the mother-bird is feeding, or brooding over her nestlings, the maternal instinct is probably stronger than the migratory; but the instinct which is the more persistent gains the victory, and at last, at a moment when her young ones are not in sight, she takes flight and deserts them.[8]

Swallows and swifts are surely not self-conscious as we are, for they would otherwise be overcome with sorrow and guilt at the consequences of their actions. It's different with human beings. We can call up images of the past and reflect on what we did. If we were in the place of the swallows, our dreams would be poisoned with images of starving, dying children.

As Darwin saw it, we need some way to resist strong, useful instincts that are dangerous if they're not kept within certain limits. Self-consciousness developed as a way of fixing an imbalance of power between different drives until, after "long habit," our "desires and passions . . . yield instantly and without a struggle to [our] social sympathies and instincts."

Why do we need to do this? The answer is easy. Humans are strong and dangerous animals when full grown, quite a match for almost any predator, but they spend years as adorable but weak and fairly incompetent children. Children need parents and parents need friends and the knowledge and wisdom of their elders. Something needs to hold the community together so that it can perpetuate itself; it takes a village to raise a child, and the job will never get done if the villagers are constantly running off. Since we have all the drives of other animals and since we need them from time to time if we're to survive, we had to develop a supplementary set of drives that keeps us at the tasks of social life by shaping, modifying, or deferring the other ones.

Darwin's account is just a little too Victorian in parts, perhaps, and he was very much committed to the idea of humans as isolated beings who have to be shaped by self-discipline so they can get along with others. It also gives too little attention to the strong family ties of other social animals, like wolves and crows. This doesn't mean that his insight has lost its value, though. On the contrary, his thoughts make even more sense if we think of self-conscious life as one part of a collective, participatory process.

Many different connections unite us with our world, and out of those innumerable connections any number of goals emerge. Where they come from doesn't make any difference; goals are goals, and logic doesn't help us choose among them. We are moved by feeling. If that were all we are and do, we would have no choice at all but to yield moment by moment to whatever goal attracted the greatest emotional charge. We would be as sinless as other animals, but we would also be as blind.

This is where the self-conscious mind comes in and its set of supplementary drives. We've given self-consciousness very little respect so far, and we've suggested very strongly that it's a kind of illusion. But it's real, and it has real power. The illusion lies only in the false way in which we think we're exercising that power. We think of the conscious self as our core identity and the organ through which we take charge of ourselves. The reality is that its voice is only one voice among many. It just operates differently from the others.

Self-consciousness is useful, in fact, and it is the royal road to real selflessness. It is at its best when it forestalls action, the way Darwin thought it did. It can teach us to be still. It can turn us away from the noisy insistence of one or another demand until we begin to hear and feel the quieter currents of our other needs and the fainter echo of the needs of others. By calling up emotionally charged images, visual or otherwise, we can hold off certain interests or goals and give others more weight. Temptation may be very strong, but it can be countered by reminding ourselves of the value and the rewards of what we're being tempted away from, the way a faithful spouse on a business trip might flip through the family photos before going down to the hotel bar. This is surely what Darwin had in mind. Thanks to self-consciousness, we have the power to silence our immediate urges, listen for our deepest desires, and open ourselves up to the silent, subtle movements of our shared life.

This often feels like the mind controlling the heart, but it would be misleading to see it that way. There's no real distinction here. Feeling and acting engage us fully, as sensitive, animate, interwoven beings. Mental, physical, rational, or emotional, they are all bodily processes. Some of them arise, connect, and find resolution without reaching consciousness. Others loop up and through conscious thinking. But they are all parts of a single network, if a clamorous and inconsistent one. No one process or group of processes dominates the others. What counts is how we position ourselves in that flow, and what perspectives we allow to open up. One of the gifts of self-consciousness is that we can actually tack and veer in the breezes of emotional life, like a skilled mariner sailing against the wind.

As Hugh Brody, who spent much time with contemporary hunting people, explains, this is also the way that many hunting bands operate—through silence, indirection, hints, and guesses:

> Joseph and his family float possibilities. "Maybe we should go to Copper Creek. Bet you lots of moose up there." Or, "Could be

caribou right now near Black Flats." Or, "I bet you no deer this time down on the Reserve. . . ." Somehow a general area is selected from a gossamer of possibilities, and from an accumulation of remarks comes something rather like a consensus. No, that is not really it: rather, a sort of prediction, a combined sense of where we *might* go "tomorrow." Yet the hunt will not have been planned, nor any preparations started, and apparently no one is committed to going.[9]

The next day, Brody adds, everyone goes off together.

The great danger is that we will use this gift the wrong way. Instead of keeping self-consciousness within proper limits, using it only to direct us back us to the richness and reality of the world, we take it for the whole of what we are and identify ourselves with it alone. We think that our conscious mind is all that we really are and that conscious thinking is all the work that really counts. Such an error is especially likely when the delicate balancing acts of egalitarian hunting life are upset and replaced by class division. There is no longer any place for the quiet opening to one another that Brody describes.

This illusion is clearly tied in with our built-in claim to be ideal agents—our unshakable belief that whatever we do is the product of our own internal free choice. As we've already seen, there is no real foundation for this belief, but we can't help ourselves from falling into it. In just the same way, we can't help identifying ourselves with our self-conscious mind. It presents itself as the whole of our mental life; it would be a paradox to be conscious of something outside consciousness. And it probably wouldn't work as a set of supplementary processes if we really knew that this was all that it was.

To be a self-conscious ideal agent, though, is to be an isolated, independent being, profoundly alone with hidden desires, hopes, and thoughts, facing a world of others who are similarly disconnected. Everyone else is a mystery at heart, an alien being whose motives and interests we can only imagine or deduce. This is the common-sense, everyday picture of who we are, shared by Dawkins, Dennett, and just about everyone else. It's also shared by the many scientists who are studying the brain, and the fit between popular ideas and this particular scientific approach helps explain the tremendous popularity of books about the brain and what contemporary neuroscience is discovering.

Self-consciousness creates the appearance of separation so masterfully that it's hard to persuade people that anything else is even conceivable. But this is an illusion, and all illusions, even necessary ones, come with a price. The price of this one is steep. Adam and Eve, the first self-conscious humans, are also the parents of the first murderer, and Cain's famous question, half excuse and half evasion—"Am I my brother's keeper?"—points out the intimate tie between our delusion of isolated self-sufficiency and crime. Our inability to feel and see our connections with our brothers and sisters is one obvious source of the cruelty and callousness that so taint our lives.

This can't be a mere intellectual mistake. Something powerful must be feeding this illusion, and the most likely candidate is fear: fear of life and its partner, death. In the world made by natural selection, no organism ranks any higher or lower than any other. The truth of our biological interwovenness is that we provide food or environmental support for disease bacteria, parasites, and predators. The truth of the perpetual flow of activity and action from one to another is that nothing is ever permanent. Our world is constantly changing, offering no place to rest, and our lives inexorably lead us to our deaths. Thanks to the foreknowledge that self-consciousness grants us, we are all too aware of these truths. It is no wonder that we would rather not face them squarely.

We look for refuge, and the refuge of first choice is not religion. It's in the self-conscious mind itself. The self seems to offer stability, identity, and control in a world where these qualities are in short supply. Longing for a still and safe place in a dangerous world, we identify with it and take it at face value. We set ourselves against everything else, which is what we really want: to find a life that's protected from life's dangers.

What happens then is that our profoundly common, shared life appears to us as something personal and private. We lay individual claim to something that is not individual at all. It's easy to pooh-pooh the pretensions of the "self-made man," easy to see that John D. Rockefeller benefited from specific social and economic structures, relied on unpaid or underpaid contributions from others, drew ideas from a common stock, and benefited from other people's decisions about what they needed or wanted. But whatever we have still seems ours by right. What success we attain seems proof of our good qualities.

There are other factors that play into this fantasy of control and individual accomplishment. The self-conscious mind not only tells us, in the teeth of the evidence, that we're ideal agents, it also comes with an ingrained tendency to justify ourselves at the expense of others. As innumerable studies have shown, we inevitably magnify our competence and virtue when we recall our past, and our automatic response to every disagreement is to assume that we are right and that others are wrong.[10]

The egotism may be inevitable a way of maintaining the necessary illusion that we're in conscious control of our own lives, but it remains pretty ugly. As psychologist Cordelia Fine warns,

> Your brain is vainglorious. It's emotional and immoral. It deludes you. It is pigheaded, secretive, and weak-willed. Oh, and it's also a bigot. This is more than a minor inconvenience.[11]

This is harsh, and it is also not really accurate; the culprit is not the brain but the gaggle of connections and responses that feed into and appear as self-consciousness.[12] All the same, Fine points to a real problem. The way we perceive and think about the world is deeply colored by the self-conscious mind's compulsion to give us an excuse for everything the we do.

Our minds miss few opportunities to remind us of our stellar virtues. All of us nurse "pet peeves." And what is a pet peeve but an opportunity for reminding ourselves of our own superiority? It makes very little objective difference in our lives that other people back into parking spaces or stand in front of their grocery carts when they check out at the supermarket. Our annoyance is just an opportunity to persuade ourselves that we are more considerate in the parking lot and make things easier for the checkout clerk. This is largely or entirely nonsense, of course, but such is the human tendency to self-justification that even years of work can't get rid of that little surge of feeling that asks, "Why don't these dopes know any better?" and implies, "Thank heavens I'm not like them."

Pet peeves fall into the minor inconvenience category. The same tendency is far more pernicious when it's combined with our belief that we are ideal agents and control our lives. Not only do we assume powers that aren't ours, the illusions of self-consciousness leave us bewildered, angry, and dangerous when it turns out that we didn't have those powers after all. We take too much credit for worldly success and we feel every failure to be a judgment on our own competence and fitness. Yet failure is inevitable, at least as long as we pursue the dream of a life under our personal control. We are tempted to think of ourselves as kings of infinite space or, at least, of those little, circumscribed spaces where we can make ourselves at home. But there is no such place; nothing and nowhere is apart from the perpetual flow of activity and coordination, destruction and rebirth. Reality inevitably shatters our illusion of control and our pretense to ideal agency.

Put all these together—the illusion of control, self-aggrandizement, the inevitability of failure, and the desire to keep safe from change and transience—and the odds are high that we will blame the mishaps of life on others. Our fellow humans are worse than mysterious creatures who can be allies one day and competitors the next. Some, at least, become enemies. (As ideal agents, after all, they must be acting just as deliberately as we are.) They may be household or family enemies, public enemies, or Evil Empires; the scale of the struggle makes no difference. To have enemies is to be stuck with endless war, psychological or physical.

Here is the origin of the human hatred of the other. Many well-intentioned people urge us to welcome and embrace human differences. They point out to us that there's nothing at all threatening about living, looking, thinking, or acting differently. But these people have it backward. Otherness does not inspire hatred. It's the need to hate someone that inspired us to invent otherness in the first place.

We have never feared or disliked people simply because they were different. Our fear and anger come out of the delusions of self-consciousness, and those delusions make it very hard to do anything with those feelings except project them on to someone else. If we're not responsible for our misfortunes and our unhappiness, then we have to find someone else to take the rap, someone who can't be associated with us in any way—someone so unlike us that we may not even want to call them human. Otherness helps us escape the responsibility for our own perfectly natural failures. Without that motivation, we wouldn't care at all what skin color, language, or religion other people came with.

This would certainly explain why religion has so often been an excuse for hatred and bloodshed. There's nothing especially dangerous about religious ideas or religious practice. As human history has shown, it's perfectly easy for adherents of different cults to live together comfortably. Religion is simply a particularly visible marker of human difference, like gender, sexual orientation, and skin color. It's an easy way of classifying people, which is what we do so we can come up with a "someone else" that we can blame for our misery. The fault is not in religion; it's in the all-too-common desire for a scapegoat.

Life is messy, and other people interfere with our plans. That's where dictatorships have their start—in dreams of perfection, a leap into cleanliness and purity. Few people have a tyrant's ruthlessness and all-encompassing ambition, of course, but that doesn't keep many of us from attacking, wheedling, forcing, demanding, cajoling, or manipulating those close to us for similar ends. The abusive husband, the smothering mother, the lover who finds fault in everything his partner is and does—all these are after perfection, too. All of them want a tidier world than the one they really live in.

We don't want to be selfish. Heaven knows, we think, we don't ask for much. But there is simply no escape from a profound and destructive selfishness as soon as we identify ourselves with the mind of self-consciousness. We can succeed as isolated egos only if we rule the world—if we knock God off his throne and take his place. That is another truth within the biblical story of the Fall. The serpent tempts Eve with the false promise that if she eats the apple, she and Adam "shall be as gods, knowing good and evil."[13] The key phrase, of course, is "ye shall be as gods."

This is the sin of Adam and Eve as Christians see it. Our ancestors weren't content to be human beings living in paradisiacal innocence. That wasn't good enough for them; no, they wanted to be like God. So do we. What poisons our lives is our obdurate insistence that we should be in charge of things, and this comes from the illusions of self-conscious ideal agency—that we are, all by ourselves, running our own lives and doing a damn good job of it.

So what can we do with this essential but treacherous thing, the self-conscious mind? That task is the great focus of most every religious tradition we know of. The spiritual teachings of many "primitive" communities, for example, tell us that the everyday world is not what it seems. Reality is hard to come at and doesn't resemble the picture we get through self-consciousness. The everyday world is intimately linked with the world of the spirits, and it cannot be understood and lived in truthfully if that lived perspective is missing.

This is only one possibility. In exceptionally subtle and sophisticated ways, the rich and complex traditions of India all deconstruct the self and self-consciousness entirely. For many Hindus, for example, ultimate reality is a unity that lies beyond all the dichotomies of self and other.[14] The real self of Hindu teaching—*atman*—is identical with ultimate reality, or *brahman*, which is the very fabric of our interwoven lives. It's the absolute stillness of contemplation and the riotous fertility of nature at once, impersonal yet playful; one traditional Indian term for reality is *lila*, or "play."

As these traditions see it, the ego of self-consciousness is different from the true self. It's a product of errors, emotional tics, and unconscious but potent habits. The root of all illusion is confusing that self with the real self of *atman*.[15] That's what yokes us to the phenomenal world and blinds us to our unity with everything else.

In the Buddhist view, there's no self at all, neither the everyday self nor *atman*. The illusion of self arises from the interaction of elements like form, feelings, perception, intentions, and consciousness. If we can realize the unreality of the self, we'll start to experience the world as an endless stream of effect after cause after effect after cause. For followers of both traditions, though, it is liberating and blissful to live fully and selflessly in that flow. It is a vastly greater version of the joy we find in cooperation and shared work. But as both traditions teach, most of the time we turn ourselves away from that fullness, trying to stop the dance of life and to freeze it into forms that happen to please us. Clinging to the grasping, arrogant, biased, and defensive self of self-consciousness is the root cause of suffering. And it's out of suffering that evil comes.

Christianity does things differently. In one way or another, it has always accepted the reality of the self-conscious mind. It just understands that mind to be a mess. Over a history of 2,000 years, its saints and sages have traced and unmasked every little evasion and strategy of defense that we humans resort to when we try to maintain our claim to being in charge. Indeed, the self of the European world is an inheritance from Christianity, and the psychological focus of the European novel and psychotherapies of all sorts grew out of these centuries of introspection and unsparing critique.

The problem, in this view, is not the self itself but the fact that it's fundamentally perverted. This, you will recall, was Paul's great theme: "the good that I would I do not: but the evil which I would not, that I do."[16] As descendants of the first man and the first woman, we cannot ever do good.

Christianity claims to repair this perversion while keeping the self intact. Salvation is surrendering our desires to God, wanting His will to be done instead of our own. Through that surrender, we are supposed to be changed completely. We are to end up with a self-conscious self that doesn't suffer from any of the illusions of such a self or the problems that come from those illusions. The Christian's screwed-up self-conscious self becomes a perfected self-conscious self.

The born-again believer can count on a stable, secure inner self as she always did before, only now her trust will be rewarded; God has fixed its tendency to sinfulness. She is still isolated from others, and her self is still her control center, but her internal boss now works in harmony with everyone else's. Since God knows what everyone really needs and cares for all life equally, doing his will makes everyone happy.

It's easy to see how the back-and-forth flow of our biological interwovenness shows up here. It's the working out of God's plan, with the deity doing the job of the mirror neurons and related systems. But Christianity also posits an abyss between creator and creation. God made us out of nothing, and he does with us what he wills. This doctrine preserves the self, but there's a price to be paid: it also severs each of those selves from their side-by-side connections, telling them to find their unity in God alone. In a way, the Christian God cuts our common world apart and then puts it back together again on different terms and with a different structure. To accept him as a transcendent creator brings about the very problem that his grace then sets out to solve.

Here, at least, science is more in harmony with the Indian tradition. Both of these teach us that the self of our experience is a fragment that we mistake for the totality and that we can't trust it. Even worse, we start down the path toward cruelty and horror the moment we take it at face value. Our real nature is found somewhere else, in the wholeness of the experience-beyond-experience where all of us live within one another. Whether we call that something the interplay of all beings or the play of *brahman* makes very little difference.

But how can we know that reality? If we can't trust what we experience and know, what can we trust? If the self of self-consciousness is an illusion, how can we learn who or what we really are? Here is where science and religion part company. Science takes place in the world of conscious subjects and thought-about objects, so it always leaves us outside the realities that it's talking about. All it can do is feed more information to the self-conscious mind. If we want to live within the reality that it points us toward, we have to leave science behind. We need some way of turning ourselves toward our real nature and opening ourselves to the world that flows in and through our bodies—that burgeons up and takes form as our bodies and minds. That's what religions provide.

Notes

1. As many biologists have pointed out, natural selection does not always lead to optimal solutions.

2. Recent research suggests that wolf packs are more commonly family groups and are more cooperative than hierarchical; that's why they're absent from this list. A recent popular work on canine behavior relies on this research; see John Bradshaw, *Dog sense: How the new science of dog behavior can make you a better friend to your pet* (New York: Basic Books, 2011).

3. This should not be seen as a triumph of nurture over nature, mind over body, or reason over emotion. Human culture and rationality are as much rooted in biology as any other aspect of our behavior; nature and nurture cannot be separated.

4. See Christopher Boehm, *Hierarchy in the forest: The evolution of egalitarian behavior* (Cambridge, MA: Harvard University Press, 1999).

5. It's worth noting that anthropologist and filmmaker Hugh Brody has glossed this story as a memory of the terrible transition from the

hunting life to farming in his *The other side of Eden: Hunters, farmers, and the shaping of the world* (New York: Macmillan, 2002).

6. Genesis 3:7–11.

7. This may be why mirror neurons seem to have developed only among primates; our ancestors grew less sensitive to these other forms of interconnection as they because increasingly self-conscious, and mirror neurons evolved as at least partial compensation.

8. Charles Darwin, *The descent of man: And selection in relation to sex* (New York: Penguin, 2004), 131. 137.

9. Hugh Brody, *Maps and dreams: Indians and the British Columbia frontier* (Vancouver: Douglas & MacIntyre, 1988), 36.

10. Amusingly, one poll revealed that 85 percent of the respondents thought they were better than average drivers. On the built-in tendency to self-aggrandizement, see Cordelia Fine, *A mind of its own: How your brain distorts and deceives* (New York: Norton, 2006).

11. Fine, *A mind of its own*, 2.

12. It is, in fact, a perfect example of the confusion between brain and mind and between mind and the active, purposeful body. The brain itself does none of the things that Fine charges—only its self-conscious aspects do.

13. Genesis 3:5.

14. The range and variety of Indian philosophy is great; this is only one viewpoint out of many. However, it would be hard to find an Indian thinker who asserts that the self-conscious mind is identical with the real self.

15. Thus, the Indian "quest for the true self" is not a search for a self resembling the one we already have, only different or better; it is leaving behind the ordinary experience of self altogether.

16. Romans 7:19.

7

This Text Will Self-Destruct

Unfortunately, this isn't the only thing that religions provide. They also feature lots of authorities who are eager to tell us who and what we really are and what we should do to fill our lives with joy and peace. This is the stock in trade of what we might call the business of religion, which is different from religious life itself, and its best-selling items are creeds—information about your real identity, the proper things to do and avoid, and the rewards and punishments for compliance and noncompliance.

There are few major religious traditions that haven't fallen into that trap. Owning or at least controlling access to the truth is a source of power, and there are always people who find that appealing. Priesthoods all over the world have perpetuated themselves by their guardianship of sacred books, their fluency in sacred languages, and their knowledge of sacred signs and rituals. But there's a deeper source of our craving for theologies and creeds that has nothing to do with the lust for power. It starts with our deep desire to have conscious, objective knowledge—to know what's out there and what's likely to come next. Knowing that death and other miseries await, we crave insight into the future, and this means that we crave knowledge of the past and the present, too.

All that we can count on for this task is the self-conscious mind, and this saddles us with yet another problem. The only thing that this mind can do is tell us stories. It's an obsessive and uncontrollable narrator.

Some of the mind's narratives are stories plain and simple, and others are stripped down so much that we call them theories or articles of faith. Whatever their form, they're attempts at explaining our past and predicting our future, nailing down what happens, and connecting those events in chains of cause and effect so that they make some kind of sense. We tell ourselves stories about friends, neighbors, strangers, the dog on the street, and the characters on television shows. Our favorite subjects, though, are our own lives. We compose narratives about who we are, where we came from, what kind of person we've been, and what kind of person we're going to become. We're always writing these self-explanatory tales, which of course are self-justifying ones, too, and we can often find ourselves listening in on an inner voice describing our life as it happens. It's as if we were all the stars of our own documentary films and came with our own off-screen narrators.

The storytelling mind is voracious. It processes every encounter and gobbles up everything that we see, hear, touch, taste, smell, think, and feel. Each passing sensation becomes a clue to secrets about ourselves, secrets that we are driven to uncover and weave into new and better stories. When we ask ourselves who we are, it's our stories that come to mind or the images that embody our stories, and it's hard to imagine that anything else might exist inside of us or that our true self might be something different.

But, as we know, our inner narrator isn't showing us the true self. It's a liar. Storytelling, even the almost storytelling that we compose through chains of images, is just another way in which the self-conscious mind conceals the real nature of our lives. In the Indian tradition this is sometimes called "monkey mind," and it makes the experience of our everyday lives as superficially similar to and as deeply different from real life as a monkey is to a human being.

Noisy and busy though it is, the monkey mind actually drains reality of much of its flavor. It labels everything that we experience with a word or image so that it can find a place in our stories. It takes a constantly changing world of unimaginable richness and slims it down into something manageable, letting go of the concrete "thisness" of every moment.

To be honest, this isn't always a bad thing. It's a necessity if we're to make use of self-consciousness at all. If we got hung up on the subtle differences between one sensation and another we could not even start to explain them. We would need a new word for every taste of ice cream and for every minute we spend with a lover, and a language that specific would be the same as gibberish. It would be like a map the same size as the land that it's mapping.

But we pay a high price for getting our stories confused with the life they try to grasp. Those tales are an activity of the separated, self-conscious self, so they leave us stuck outside the world and even outside ourselves, at one remove from the concrete, specific, and indescribable truth found within our bodily lives. Even if we're not filming ourselves or tweeting about our busy lives, we weigh and evaluate our level of enjoyment at an amusement park, the intensity of our response to a favorite singer's latest concert, and how satisfactory our orgasm was. We figure out how we got to where we are right now and how this moment makes sense in terms of our past—even as that moment vanishes. We worry or take pleasure in the thought of what will come. We rarely if ever simply live.

Through our image making and storytelling, we clutch at the passing shapes of a process that embraces the entire world, fondly imagining that its truth isn't running through our hands like sand. We cut ourselves off from reality by fragmenting it, freezing the wreckage, and forging a self from the rubble. The task is all the more endless and desperate because it starts from a betrayal of reality, the separation of a seamless world into subjects, all of them lost in a sea of objects.

Yet reality still shows itself to us. Every now and then we find ourselves effortlessly involved with one another or fully present within a few moments of an otherwise ordinary day. These brief glimpses of the unbounded and indescribable reality of the world bring us so much joy and such a feeling of richness and depth that we want more than anything else for them to return.

If we're thinking only in terms of the monkey mind, we'll be all too happy to believe the peddlers of creeds and spiritual secrets when they tell us that they have the answers we're seeking—about the nature of the divine, our relationship with it, how we can make that relationship better, and where to go so that we can plant our feet once again on the blissful shores of reality. We've been living our lives through stories, and this kind of religion doesn't ask us to stop. It just asks us to believe that its stories are based on more accurate information and produce better results than our old ones. Who wouldn't want that? If real life is a lost treasure, we're eager to grasp at any treasure map we come across.

Alas, the treasure map of religious discourse is just as delusive as a map to Captain Kydd's gold. We can't escape the world of theories and stories by learning new and improved theories and stories. The truly religious in every tradition understand this. The medieval theologian Thomas Aquinas wrote hundreds of volumes setting out what has become the basis for Catholic theology, but he had a vision after saying mass a few months before he died and refused to write any more, saying, "All that I have written seems to me like so much straw compared to what I have seen and what has been revealed to me."[1]

As Thomas found out, religious discourse is no different from any other kind of discourse. It gets confused with and falsifies the living reality that it started out from. To find the truth, we need to step outside our pose as subjective observers of an objective reality and disentangle our sense of self from stories—ours or anyone else's. Yet how can we do that without the very stories and ideas that trap us? How can anyone point us toward the real and show us what to do without using the untrustworthy tools of the monkey mind?

One time-honored technique is tricking the story machine, not ignoring or condemning it but turning it against itself. Many great spiritual teachers, past and present, have used strange kinds of discourse that frustrate or undercut our attempts at making sense of the words themselves. They tell us truths and then tell us contradictory truths. They show us a thousand different supreme beings and worship each one in turn. To outsiders this may look like nonsense—but that's just the point. If "sense" is a matter of stories and theories, reality can only be approached through non-sense.

Koans, the questions that students of Zen are given to ponder, are classic examples of self-destructive discourse. Two of the best known are "What was your face before you were born?" and "What is the sound of one hand clapping?" Others resemble pointless anecdotes. In the first koan discussed in an old Zen text, *The Gateless Gate*, a monk asks a master, "Does a dog have Buddha nature?" and the master shouts, "No!"[2]

Koans are not as crazy as they sound, however. Each is disconcerting in a different way, but all of them are meant to do the same work, which is to get the student to see that the conscious mind and all its theories are completely useless if we want to live knowingly within the real world. *The Gateless Gate* explains,

> Concentrate your whole body . . . into the Question; day and night, without ceasing, hold it before you. But do not take it as nothingness, nor as the relative "not", of "is" and "is not." It must be like a red-hot iron ball which you have gulped down and which you try to vomit, but cannot.
>
> All the useless knowledge, all the wrong things you have learned up to the present—throw them away! After a certain period of time, this striving will come to fruition naturally, in a state of internal and external unity. As with a dumb man who has had a dream, you will know it yourself, and for yourself only. Suddenly your whole activity is put into motion and you can astonish the heavens above and shake the earth beneath. . . . You meet a Buddha? You kill him! A master of Zen? You kill him![3]

(I am using R. H. Blyth's translation of the Japanese version, the *Mumonkan*.)

As this commentary explains, the student has to keep struggling with the koan until he fully grasps the futility of any rational approach to the question. He—they were almost always men until recently—needs to ask himself the question over and over. Each partial answer and every attempt at evading the problem or defining it away gets the same response: an angry word or a beating from the master. By forcing himself to struggle with the koan in the right way, the student sets his self-conscious mind on the path to a complete meltdown.

Once this happens, the student really and truly leaves conscious thinking aside. The "answer" comes spontaneously because the "problem" no longer exists. The particular answer is not important at all; there can be any number of answers. All of them are correct as long as they come directly out of the student's experience. On the other hand, an answer that suggests an explanation has to be wrong, because real experience can't be described or explained. This is why this knowledge is like the dream of a man who cannot communicate it. It is the student's knowledge and his alone, and once he comes to such a realization, all the Buddhist scriptures and the sermons of the wisest teachers are useless and even harmful.

But we should notice that the commentary warns against taking the problem "as nothingness, [or] as the relative 'not', of 'is' and 'is not.'" The koan isn't a nonproblem, and its answer isn't the discovery that nothing can be known. Denying knowledge keeps us from experience just as surely as our addiction to the monkey mind does. It slathers a warm thick gravy of everything-is-the-same-as-everything-else over life, which is as big a betrayal of reality as the worst and most schematic theory. It's just another claim to conceptual knowledge. It just happens to take the form of a positive assertion that knowledge is impossible.

There is such a thing as real knowledge, but it's not attained by thinking. And though thinking is dangerous when we concentrate on the ideas instead of the things that inspired them, it doesn't have to be a waste of time. "What was your face before you were born?" turns us toward the notion of a self without any narratives—experience before it gets tangled up in self versus everything else. The sound of one hand clapping is, at one level, an act without context and is as absurd as our belief that our actions can be understood as ours alone. Nor is the monk's question about dogs a stupid one. It's a good, serious, theological inquiry. Translated into Christian ideas, it's like the question, "Does a dog have a soul?" The monk might be eager to know what his ethical duties are to dogs in general in the way that Christians sometimes base their view of animal rights on whether other animals have immortal souls.

You can come up with a code of morals by working that way, and your code might help you live more gently and lovingly among people and dogs. That kind of rational and self-conscious thinking is useful and may even be necessary for everyday life. But Zen—like all religious traditions—is concerned with reality, not with usefulness. The monk was asking a reasonable but abstract question about a theological dog, a conceptual dog, a dog of no particular color and breed. Whatever thoughts we can derive from abstract dogness, the real dog always slips away while we're thinking them, with or without the real Buddha nature. And we're really interested in the real dog, who like a real person stands in front of us and deserves to be seen whole and clearly.

There seems to be a paradox here. The student's insight into reality is said to do two things that at first blush are diametrically opposed to one another. It puts him in a place where what he knows cannot be communicated to anyone else. He can no longer discuss his thoughts about the Buddha nature of dogs with his friends or convince them of their truth. He's placed himself outside the public world of shared language and ideas. As a result of the very same process, though, he is supposed to be more profoundly connected with the world. Buddhist literature (and Hindu literature as well) is full of claims that enlightened sages can see deeply into the hearts and minds of others.

This is a paradox, though, only if we believe that our real ties with others are made through words or other symbols. It seems that way, of course, but it also seems to us that our bodies are nothing but the mostly obedient servants of the all-commanding mind. Now that we know that this isn't true, it should be easy to see that intimacy with others isn't about exchanging information. Our deep conversations tie us together because talking back and forth helps us open to one another. The words can be anything; far more important is the growing ease with which we see and hear one another. That's why working silently with someone can also start a friendship. So can any coordinated movement, which is one reason that dancing is such a common form of courtship and why we recognize in the great romantic duets between Fred Astaire and Ginger Rogers that we're watching two people falling deeply in love. Allowing yourself to move beyond language and concept doesn't cut you off from everyone else. It can—or at least should—bring you closer to the real grounds of our connection.

We can't do justice to the koan in a page or two. I bring it up here as one use of language in religion that turns on itself and forces us to see that its subject is something that cannot be talked or written about. The *Tao te ching*, which was written long before Zen emerged, does this explicitly. Right from the start, it warns us that it can't talk about or give a name to its subject:

> The Dao that can be described in language is not the constant Dao; the name that can be given it is not its constant name.[4]

But there are other strategies to keep the student from mistaking the words for the indescribable truth. In oral cultures, the very way that religious ideas are taught and discussed incorporates the insight that nothing the teacher says can be literally true.

In communities without writing, the most common way of teaching and thinking about fundamental issues is to tell stories—myths, we call them. You might think that this is just the wrong way to outsmart the storyteller of our conscious mind. But myth telling lets us indulge our natural tendency to explain things through narrative and then shows us that we can explain the same things by an infinite number of different narratives. This is the key. Living by myth shows you that there are many true stories, but reality itself is always a step beyond our grasp—many ways of living truthfully but no truth that we can enunciate and stick to.

There's no way to put together all the myths from a community so that they don't contradict themselves. No two people can agree on the correct version of any story, and few myth tellers are interested in harmonizing differences or arguing over which version is closer to the truth. "Yes," they might say, "I've heard that there are people who tell the story that way. I'm just telling you how *I* heard it." Did Raven made the world when it was all water? Did animals dredge up mud and make the world so that the woman falling from the sky would have a place to land? Did Coyote and Fox sing it into existence? Are any of these true? Or are they all partial but illuminating aspects of something else?[5]

Those who tell and hear these stories see nothing wrong in giving accounts with different plot details, altering important facts like who's related to whom, and borrowing elements of one story and dropping them down in the midst of another. Yet they insist that the stories embody profound truths. These are different versions of the same story, somehow, and all of them are equally true—whatever that could possibly mean.

This makes myth telling seem like the sort of thing that only "primitive" people could be satisfied with. But we think this only if we judge myths by the standards of the self-conscious mind, which is just what the myth tellers are trying to get us to lay aside. People in oral cultures are neither primitive nor stupid. They know that the real truth of myth can't be separated from the fact that every retelling is false or inadequate. Indeed, it *depends* on that fact. We're tempted to grab on to the story we just heard and think that we possess the one true account of things, but the myths won't let themselves be used that way. They have to be told over and over again and differently until we cure ourselves of our attachment to facts and stories and look beyond the myth to what the myth shows.[6]

The pianist Artur Schnabel once said that great music is music that's greater than it can be played. The myth tellers' truth is great in the same way. Each telling will offer a few perspectives on something that we can never fully grasp or even refer to as a thing. The teller does not claim to produce anything more. Every telling of a myth is both a failure and a success because there can be no fixed version of the story, no telling—only retelling.

Through an inner logic or necessity, myths retell *themselves*. This modesty is how they point to the ungraspable. In this way, at least, myth telling is reminiscent of the practice of Zen. Like the absurdity of the koan, the fact that each retelling is literally untrue undermines our habit of mistaking explanations for things.

This brings us to a very important question. Can myths—or any religious text or practice—make any claim to truth at all? Put in a different way, does the notion of truth have any meaning once we abandon the logic and theories of the self-conscious mind? Surely most myth tellers believe that their stories are true. There are always going to be people who take them as literal truth in every possible sense, and it is possible to experience them as literally true. But to accept different accounts as valid while sticking with your own version suggests a different standard than that of factual truth.

There are at least two kinds of truth. The first, truth in the lawyer's and the scientist's sense, is propositional truth. It's worked out in the terms of the self-conscious mind only, which lives in and is bound by language and logic. Under these rules, the truth of one theory or story excludes all its rivals.

The second kind of "truth" is not subject to this law. In this sense of the word, there can be many different, overlapping, or even contradictory true stories. What these have in common is that all of them point you toward something real. A story is true if it does that. It's false if it leads you astray.

The sages of religions like Zen, Taoism, and Hinduism, like the myth tellers, aren't fundamentally concerned with giving you factual information about the world. (As one Balinese Hindu asked his German guest, "Do you want to know whether the story is true or merely whether it occurred?"[7]) They're trying to suggest what the world is like, how you might act if you want to live in its reality, and what real life might feel like. To do this truthfully, their teachings have to direct you past their words and toward the real forces and processes that are at work in the world, a world that seamlessly includes ourselves along with everything else. When they move you in that direction, they place you in a nonsubjective relationship to an objective reality.

By this standard, they are all true teachings whether or not they're true in the first sense. I mean this seriously. Just because reality can't be described or pinned down doesn't mean that it doesn't exist. The second way of using "truth" and "true" is just as impersonal and rigorous as the first. It doesn't depend on social agreement or personal whim any more than the first one does. You can't just make something up and find it so pleasant that you proclaim it to be true for you. There is no "personal reality." There is only reality, without any qualification.[8]

This, of course, is why novels and films can be true and why images can show us reality. The two kinds of truth work in different ways, though—a novel is no longer true if we think that the characters are real—and when we seek these different kinds of truth we act and live differently, too. The first kind of truth starts from our stories about experiences and it's verified when it predicts the stories that we will generate about other experiences. This is the scientific kind of truth and the one that the makers of creeds aspire to. The second kind of truth opens us up and out to the world so that we become ever more attentive to the life in and around us.

Myth tellers show us the hidden activity of the world, constantly giving us hints of those connection that unite us with everything else. Their stories work like the dye injected into a vein to make our blood vessels show up on an X-ray. The myth world is *our* world, except that the invisible can be seen along with the visible. That is why it is filled with impossibilities.

As the paleontologist Jean Clottes says in Werner Herzog's mesmerizing *Cave of Forgotten Dreams*, the myth world is one of fluidity and permeability. The world appears to be populated by separate, skin-bounded people and animals who move about in apparently empty space, but myth tellers know that this is an illusion. We are totally woven into a world that stands outside and against us in appearance only. In the landscape of myth the illusions of solidity and separation are dispelled. Our profound embraidedness comes to the surface and almost anything can become anything else.

A man falls in love with a she-bear and eventually becomes a bear himself. Coyote plants sticks in the ground, and the next morning they are people, complaining about the fleas. (He regrets his creation instantly and sends them away.) Feathers are snow. Weather puts on the skin of a wren and becomes a cumulus cloud. In the skin of a Steller's jay, he is a wide blue sky, and clothed in sapsucker's feathers, he is the bright red sunrise. All things are endlessly being transformed, leaving nothing permanent but change.

Does this mean that the distinctions are illusions and that everything is purely and simply one? Not at all. Myths don't fall into the trap that *The Gateless Gate* warns against. They don't pour the everything-is-one gravy over experience, and they won't let us sit comfortably in a world of yes and no and is and is not. The myth world is one and many and whole and divided, both at once; with equal justice, we could say that it is, at the same time, neither one nor many, neither whole nor divided. Myths acknowledge that we live in two worlds at once—that we are truly ourselves only in a world where we cannot stay for long.

Every division is always being overcome, and as that happens the division always reappears. The one reality appears only in separation, which is as necessary as it is illusory. The animal/people of the myth time are just like us, but they must not be confused with the animals and the people of everyday life. The way people talk about Old Man Coyote, the trickster god of much of western North America, shows this deliberate blurring. Is he a man? Is he a coyote? In reality he is both of these, and in reality he is neither. If we think of animals and people as separate, we cannot think of him at all, but the whole idea of Old Man Coyote loses its meaning if we think they are the same. Old Man Coyote is a koan in himself. To meet him in the flesh, we must understand for ourselves—not just intellectually—that the world is betrayed by the categories of the conscious mind but that we can't do away with those categories, either.

Myths keep us from reducing reality to human concepts, including the concepts found in the myths themselves. They do this effortlessly; it's a simple consequence of the way that they are told and listened to. Unfortunately, it's very hard to carry the truthfulness of myth from an egalitarian and oral culture into a literate one with a priesthood. Writing mummifies myth. Living stories become dead, fixed texts. Their power is still there, deep down in the words, but it gets harder and harder for us to look past the surface and find it. Instead, we're apt to get lost in the surface itself.

The problem isn't confined to fundamentalist Christians. It's endemic; any sacred text becomes a subject for logical elaboration. The very notion of God carries the same danger. Once we come up with an almighty god, it's just too easy to think that we've got firm knowledge about him and that we consequently know something about reality itself. All talk about divine ineffability is undermined by the assertion that there is "a God." We may act in all humility, and we may think with all sincerity that our ideas reflect the reality we invoke by that title, but we're really papering over reality with our own ideas and worshipping our own thoughts writ large. This is exactly what the Bible means by idolatry.

Paradoxically, one of the best ways to escape idolatry is to worship real idols. That, at least, is how images can work in most of the religious traditions of India. By giving a diversity of gods name and form, Indian tradition allows philosophically inclined worshippers to think and talk about Ganesh, Krishna, Kali, or Shiva without falling into the error of thinking that they've said anything final about the universe itself.

Hinduism is often thought of as polytheistic, and it certainly gives that impression. One traditional estimate is that there are 330 million gods, and by any count the number of divinities is overwhelming. Yet this riot of divinity is misleading in the same way that the incoherence of myth is misleading. The 330 million gods are *supposed* to make your head spin, and the stories about the gods are more truthful *because* they contradict one another.

For many worshippers, the image of a god at a temple or household shrine carries the presence of an immensely powerful friend or protector. To others, the teeming pantheon of gods, demons, and spirits is an annoying concession to an ignorant public that cannot grasp the pure monotheism that lies behind the images. Taken on their own terms, however, the deities of India embody a powerful and sophisticated understanding of the problem of showing something about the divine without falsifying it by turning it into information.[9]

As the myths of oral communities do, the Hindu pantheon invites us into a world where the logic of noncontradiction doesn't exist. At various times, Surya, Vishnu, Krishna, Shiva, the Goddess, or Ganesh may be praised as the one supreme deity. They can't be used to compare one thing with another, and they can't be assembled into a system. This proliferation of divinity turns us aside before we can start labeling reality with abstract nouns like "justice" and "mercy." We can say that Lakshmi is merciful or that Vishnu acts for justice, but there are other supreme gods with different attributes, so it's clear that doing this doesn't tell us anything ultimately true about what is ultimately real.

Like a fractal pattern, the multiplicity of Indian gods is reproduced in the gods themselves. Devi, the Goddess, can appear as Shiva's wife Parvati, a passionate ascetic who both challenges and complements her equally passionate and ascetic husband. But she is also Lakshmi at the feet of her sleeping husband Vishnu, submissively seated by the most impure part of his body like an old-fashioned Indian wife. She is Durga, the great conqueror and the dispeller of illusions, the divine mother, formed from the combined power of all the gods and therefore superior to them all, the creative force who generates the universe out of herself, present, she tells us, "in all knowledge and in all women." She is Kali, naked except for a skirt of severed arms and legs and a necklace made of severed heads, guzzling hot blood and dancing so wildly at slaughter that the other gods have to stop her before she devours the entire world. She is the queenly and beautiful Raja Rajeshwari, the divinity of the Sri Vidya tradition of South India. None of these can be squared with one another in any conventional way, but they are all Devi.

Even a single aspect of a single divinity may be described in self-contradictory terms. Kali, especially as depicted in Bengal, is both destroyer and nurturing mother. Durga tells us that she is *maya*—illusion—and the remedy for *maya* at the same time. Shiva is free of all human desires; he is not only a god but an ascetic, preferring a blissfully silent existence meditating in his home on Mount Kailash. Yet his sexuality is so potent that the other gods are forced to interrupt him and Parvati lest their lovemaking destroy the universe. On another hand—Hindu gods are blessed with many other hands—Shiva is complete in himself. He cannot truly desire anything or anyone. This is hard on Parvati, who is a human incarnation of a god with human emotions and needs. And on the fourth hand, Shiva's grief at the death of his first wife Sati is so cataclysmic that it, too, must be stopped. He flies around the earth weeping, her dead body in his arms, scalding the earth with every teardrop. The other gods cut Sati's body away bit by bit until the sorrowing god is free of his burden and his feelings subside.

These contradictions, so reminiscent of the contradictions in the myth world, are all to the good. The reality of our split lives is just as contradictory; we are both divided and whole, exiled yet always at home. The cultural awareness that reality constantly negates itself and resists any and all formulation may be why myth telling as a sacred practice still thrives in India. The holy books of India are filled with stories—excellent stories, like those in the gigantic, magical, and tragic tale of the *Mahabharata*. These stories are as alive today as ever. The poet and translator P. Lal said of the *Mahabharata* that its "characters still walk the Indian streets, its animals populate our forests, its legends and myths haunt and inspire the Indian imagination, its events are the disturbing warp and woof of our age." Yet these stories survive not so much because they're thought of as being literally true but because they resist being embalmed in theology.[10]

The tales of the Indian traditions aren't simply good yarns that leave us entertained yet none the wiser. Although the gods do a fine job of tripping us up before we turn reality into a story or a theory, they don't tell us that reality is a mystery and that we consequently can't know anything about it at all. Like all good myths, they show us what they can't or won't tell.

In the stories about the gods, we glimpse what reality is really like—not all of it, of course, but some aspect of it that helps us on our way toward encountering it ourselves. Some gods, like Krishna in his enchanting and passionate youth, show us the inherent delight of life, love, sex, and boundless energy. (The adult Krishna of the

Mahabharata is much more complex and disturbing.) Others, more compellingly perhaps, acknowledge the darkness that we spend our lives evading, the inevitability of death and sorrow and the terrible truth that at one and the same time we are little lower than the angels and an excellent source of nutrition for other life forms. The scholar David Kinsley wrote of the terrifying Kali,

> Sickness, old age, and death are the very texture of life, and to think otherwise is to remain hopelessly deluded. To live is by definition to participate in these realities. This is the way things are, and nothing can be done to change it. . . . The image of Kali in the cremation ground or as a shrunken, wrinkled, skeletal hag fastens one's attentions on those aspects of life that cannot be avoided and must eventually result in pain, sorrow, and lamentation. . . . Meditation on Kali, confrontation of her, even the slightest glimpse of her, restores man's hearing, thus enabling or forcing a keener perception of things around him. Confronted with the vision of Kali, he begins to hear, perhaps for the first time, those sounds he has so carefully censored in the illusion of his physical immortality: "the wail of all the creatures, the moan of pain, and the sob of greed, and the pitiful cry of little things in fear."[11]

Shiva, too, can bring us face-to-face with this unacceptable reality. Like Kali, who is sometimes shown dancing on his prostrate body, Shiva is fond of the cremation ground, and as befits someone eternally contemplative, he points to the pointlessness of any conclusion we can draw about anything at all. In the words of Namita Gokhale,

> The divine madman, the ash-besmeared destroyer of the ego, of illusion and comfortable appearances, is not an easy or convenient god to worship. He offers the consolation of neither moral relativism nor absolutism. There is no code of conduct, no easy categorizing, no promise of heaven or hell, only the uncompromising view of man and his god as a naked beggar, besmeared with the ash that portends both his mortality and immortality, a grinning skull on the palm of his hand.[12]

To focus on such potent images and accept what they show us is to face and surrender our fears and our evasions of life, bit by bit.

The power of the stories and images of the gods is that they reveal how you live when you see the world as it really it. The gods have no illusions. They're fully aware of reality, and through their eyes we can see what it's like to live there. (If you'd prefer a more scientific approach, one can say that the stories about gods show us what it's like to live without concepts and with full attention.) The Sanskrit word usually translated as "god" is *deva*, and it originally meant "shining one"; the gods glow with the luminosity of reality itself.

Indian tradition has transmitted an awesome image of Vishnu in the interval between worlds as an infant lost in play, alone on an island in an endless sea.[13] We are ultimately not separate from him. All the universe is the play of body to body, endless coordination and effortless interaction, perpetual creation and destruction, in which we ourselves participate and of which we ourselves can become aware. When we do that we see the world as divine—the word descends from *deva*—and we, too, shine with the light of existence itself.

It is a blinding radiance. The famous image of the dancing Shiva is meant to convey it in all its glory and terror. Dancing on a dwarfed figure representing ignorance, the god simultaneously destroys and creates the universe. He is surrounded by the fires of cremation and beats the drum whose sound brings the world into existence. His matted hair flies wildly out as he dances, but his face is impassive and calm; things are as they are, and they inspire no pain, fear, or longing in him. And he beckons us with a gesture of reassurance and points to his foot, where one touches a god or a teacher in loving submission.

It is hard for many of us to accept his invitation. As we saw in the previous chapter, our fear of death and pain is the biggest obstacle to our experiencing the world as it is. We may know that Shiva is showing us reality, but we cannot feel our way to dancing with him. We stand to lose too much.

Yet Kali shows us this too, more directly perhaps because she addresses us more personally. As Kinsley points out,

Pain and sorrow are woven into the texture of man's life so thoroughly that to deny them is ultimately futile and foolish. For man to realize the fullness of his being, for man to exploit his potential as a human being, he must finally accept this dimension of existence. Kali's boon is freedom, the freedom of the child to revel in the moment, and it is won only after confrontation with death. . . . To ignore death, to pretend that one's ego is the center of things, is to provoke Kali's mocking laughter. To confront or accept death, on the contrary, is to realize a mode of being that can delight and revel in the play of the gods. To accept one's mortality is to be able to act superfluously, to let go, to be able to sing, dance, and shout. To win Kali's boon is to become childlike, to be flexible, open, and naive like a child.[14]

It is not without justice that the dreadful Kali is also the great mother. Like any loving parent, she leads her children to see and understand the world outside the safety of the womb in all its beauty and horror. That is the knowledge that gives them the strength to live as real adults. The terrifying encounter with Kali and the reality she reveals is ultimately liberating.

Different gods and goddesses appeal to different people. Each is likely to offer only a partial view of an ungraspable reality, of course, but this partiality is not a fault. All the gods live within the totality of things. The ones we are drawn to show us our own weaknesses and failings. They reveal to us the specific fears and delusions that bar each one of us from experiencing reality, and devoting oneself to one's chosen god dispels those precise fears and delusions. The unbridled joy of Krishna in his earthly paradise of Vrindavan may call to the emotionally cloistered, while Durga's maternal care and guidance can speak to those who have felt unloved and unmoored. Understanding a god is a way of understanding oneself, and submitting to her power is a way of freeing oneself from the particular poisons that keep one from living in the one unknowable but indubitably real world.

Here, it should be clear, is where language is obviously useless. If we want to learn from the gods, we have to take ourselves past the point where we can be taught anything by words. They are not meant to be objects of study. They must become living presences, and those presences have to be invoked and cultivated for them to show us what they see. In other words, they exist in and through religious practices, and it is to the world of religious practice that we now turn.

Notes

1. This story has been handed down from Thomas's earliest biographers.
2. R. H. Blyth, *Zen and Zen classics*, vol. 4, *The Mumonkan* (Tokyo: Hokuseido Press, 1966), 22.
3. Blyth, *Zen and Zen classics*, 32.
4. *The classic of the Way and virtue: A new translation of the Tao-te ching of Laozi as interpreted by Wang Bi*, trans. Richard John Lynn (New York: Columbia University Press, 1999), 51. This is in the traditional ordering; there is some variation and scholarly debate on the original one.
5. As Jaime De Angulo was told, "maybe the whole thing just never happened. . . . And maybe it did happen but everybody tells it different. People often do that, you know"; *Indian tales* (New York: Hill & Wang, 1953), 240.
6. As the novelist Tim Parks notes, "In *The Marriage of Cadmus and Harmony* Roberto Calasso shows that one of the defining characteristics of a living mythology was that its many stories, always so excitingly tangled together, always had at least two endings, often 'opposites'— the hero dies, he doesn't die, the lovers marry, they don't marry. It was only when myth became history, as it were, that we began to feel there should be just one 'proper' version, and set about forgetting the alternatives," http://www.nybooks.com/blogs/nyrblog/2012/mar/13/why-finish-books/.
7. Peter Bichsel, *Der Leser, Das Erzälen: Frankfurter Poetik-Vorlesungen* (Darmstadt: Hermann Luchterhand, 1982), trans. in Balagangadhara, S. N., quoted in S. N. Balagangadhara, *"The heathen in his blindness": Asia, the West, and the dynamic of religion* (New Delhi: Manohar, 2005), 368.
8. This obviously creates questions of verification, but the first kind of truth is just as problematic. The truth of a scientific theory isn't

determined by how well it "fits the facts." Ptolemaic astronomy fit the then-observable facts better than Copernicus's theory, but Copernicus was closer to the truth. A good theory is a fruitful one, and until we see how fruitful it is when it's compared to its rivals, we can't say which one is "true." This is the same test that Jesus suggested should be applied to prophets when he said, "By their fruits shall ye know them."

9. The Indian worshipper has no difficulty in combining any number of these attitudes and rightly so; these theories are themselves best read as myths.

10. Quoted by Sashi Tharoor, "Timeless epic," *The Hindu*, January 2, 2005, magazine section. One of the tragedies of political Hinduism is the transformation of mythlike stories into canonical tales of an imagined past, remaking Indian tradition as if it were Christianity with its claim to factual truth.

11. David R. Kinsley, *The sword and the flute: Kali & Krsna, dark visions of the terrible and the sublime in Hindu mythology* (Berkeley: University of California Press, 1975), 139, 141.

12. Namita Gokhale, *The book of Shiva* (New Delhi: Penguin Books India, 2001), 84–85.

13. The original text is in the *Markandeya Purana*, and the image is found in Indian art, but the story is most easily available in the perhaps over-poetical version in Heinrich Robert Zimmer, *Myths and symbols in Indian art and civilization* (Princeton, NJ: Princeton University Press, 1972), 42–43.

14. Kinsley, *The sword and the flute*, 144–45.

8

The Body Speaks, the Mind Listens

Religious practice comes in many forms, and some of them look strange or even pathological to outsiders. Christians watching the ritual processions of Shi'ite penitents whipping themselves with chains often think of horror films about the Black Death. The Chinese communists had similar thoughts when they saw pious Buddhists circling the holy city of Lhasa by prostrating themselves at every step. Even religious people often rush to distance themselves from such practices, explaining—and perhaps believing themselves—that they're remnants of primitive superstitions that we modern people have thankfully left aside.

The sun dance of the Plains Indians also makes people shudder. The flesh of the dancers is pierced and skewers or animal claws are inserted. A rope or thong is strung from the claws or skewers to the top of a pole in the center of the sun dance lodge, and at the climax of the dance the dancers tear themselves free. It sounds barbaric and is certainly excruciating, and for decades the sun dance was prohibited in both the United States and Canada. But the dancers know why they torture themselves. In the book *Lame Deer, Seeker of Visions*, the Lakota holy man John Fire Lame Deer (Tahca Ushte) defended the dance, turning it into a challenge to his largely Christian audience:

> Do you not in your churches pray to one who is "pierced," nailed to a cross for the sake of his people? No Indian ever called a white man uncivilized for his beliefs or forbade him to worship as he pleased.

The difference between the white man and us is this: You believe in the redeeming powers of suffering, if this suffering was done by someone else, far away, two thousand years ago. We believe that it is up to every one of us to help each other, even through the pain of our bodies. Pain to us is not "abstract," but very real. We do not lay this burden on our god, nor do we want to miss being face to face with the spirit power. It is when we are fasting on the hilltop, or tearing our flesh at the sun dance, that we experience the sudden insight, come closest to the mind of the Great Spirit. Insight does not come cheaply, and we want no angel or saint to gain it for us and give it to us secondhand.[1]

The visionary experiences of the dance can be so great that the pain, intense though it must be, is a small price to pay.

Self-inflicted pain is not unusual. It finds a place in just about every religious tradition that we know of and even survives in mainstream American religious life though in very weakened form; the all-day fast on Yom Kippur and giving up sweets for Lent are examples. But this universality is not evidence that religion is inherently neurotic or the refuge of those consumed with self-hatred. Pain—the real thing, not the symbolic variety—has deep transformational powers.

We might come to terms with the power of religious pain through a practice with which we're more familiar: the vision quest. Something of a cliché now in sports like wrestling, the term has become so popular that one group has registered the form "VisionQuest" as a trademark. VisionQuest®, should you be curious, is a "comprehensive national youth services organization . . . providing innovative intervention services to at-risk youth and families." It offers "physically and psychologically challenging activities designed to penetrate defensiveness, build confidence and foster a sense of positive accomplishment."

The real vision quest, which Lame Deer referred to as "fasting on the hilltop," is something else. There are no counselors, your friends have to leave before you're done, and it's designed to foster a sense of absolute powerlessness instead of positive accomplishment. It is only when you leave everything behind that you can receive what the spirits offer.

Visions come after a terrifying, disorienting journey that requires long preparation and self-discipline. More than a century ago the unfortunate Crow warrior Two Leggings, who had participated in the sun dance but had been given no reward for his pain, decided to fast at a sacred location with others similarly eager to receive power and a spirit guide. One of his friends helped him cut off a piece of his own flesh, and Two Leggings "held the piece up to the sky, and told the Great Above Person that [he] wished for some animal to eat this and help [him] receive a powerful medicine."[2] After two nights of prayer and fasting he heard a noise. He thought in his fear that the Thunderbird, the area's resident spirit, was approaching, but to his relief it turned out to be only a hailstorm.

Then, on the morning of the last day of his quest, he had a dream:

> A man appeared above the horizon and a voice which I could not locate spoke to me. The man was waist-high above the horizon where the sun would soon rise. A hawk perched on a hoop on his head. Something red in the right side of the man's hair grew larger and finally colored the entire sky. A streak of the brightest red went up the middle. The man asked if I knew the name of the bird on his head. I lay still without speaking. He said the name of the bird was The Bird Above All The Mountains. In the future, he said, people would hear about me all over the earth. Then I learned my vision man's song: "Thank you. A long time going to be a chief. Thank you again."[3]

Two Leggings never attained the chiefly status that he desperately longed for, but as he told the story of his life to a researcher from the Museum of American Indian, he added, "I also think he was telling me that one day a white man would be sent to write my life in a book so that people all over the earth would read my story."[4]

The vision quest brings together pain and isolation. Both of these are potent agents of change, but they work in almost opposite ways.

The sensation of pain is so intense and floods our nervous system with so many signals that it's hard to focus on anything else. The attention of the self-conscious mind contracts. Isolation, on the other hand, eliminates the boundaries that keep our thoughts and feelings within a comfortable range. Deprived of the feedback that we get from familiar routines, sights, sounds, and surroundings, the mind begins to expand. Self and other begin to blur.

In his book *Sacred Pain* the scholar Ariel Glucklich explains these extreme religious practices on the basis of recent neurological research. "If you scourge your body repeatedly," he writes, "the sensory over-stimulation would not eradicate your thoughts, sense perceptions, and so forth. But your experience of being a self, an agent who undergoes these perceptions and thoughts, would gradually disappear, until it seemed that these belonged to someone or something else."[5] Intense pain or intense stimulation of any kind shrinks the sense of self; we seem to vanish. (The head-banging adolescents at the front row of a heavy metal concert are seeking just this kind of experience.) Sensory deprivation, on the other hand, leads to an expansion of mental experience, often in the form of hallucinations.

Glucklich's ideas suggest how the vision quest can open the way toward transformative experience. The combination of pain and isolation sets our attention free of both internal and external moorings. The world expands beyond our ability to think about it, and at the very same time our sense of self fades. We let go enough to offer ourselves to the spirit animals as their food, and the world becomes strange enough that we can see those animals walking abroad and speaking to us.

This would be merely an anthropological detail except for one thing. In some important respects, the vision quest takes us closer to reality than we get in everyday life. The world may not be filled with spirit helpers and men with hawks on their heads, but the paths through which beings are connected are just as elusive as they are. In a strong sense, the world is nothing but the play of those connections, and the intimate relationship between the seeker and her powerful and all-knowing spirit companion is a good metaphor for the way those connections run. As we've seen, we ourselves are nothing like the ideal agents that we think we are. Neither masters of our fate nor captains of our soul, we are parts of a complex dance who are moved as much as we move ourselves. The self enthralled by pain, open to the inspiration and assistance of spirits, has more in common with the real self than the self of ordinary self-consciousness does.

We don't have to torture ourselves physically to achieve similar states. Hindu and Buddhist temples and Catholic and Orthodox churches have long been designed to dazzle and awe the worshipper, and the combined effects of incense, music, statues or icons, brilliant costumes, and spectacular architecture can affect even nonbelievers. We are still humbled by Notre Dame in Paris or the cathedral at Chartres, and we can easily imagine how overcome a medieval peasant would have been by the sights, smells, and sounds of high mass in a Gothic cathedral—especially after many hours of standing on the stone floor. (There were no chairs or pews in medieval churches.)

Song and dance are also powerful tools to put the self-conscious self to one side, especially when they're carried on for a long time. The music for religious rituals is often repetitive, partly because nothing breaks your concentration as much as fumbling through the hymnal and partly because each repetition can focus your attention more tightly on the music itself. The call-and-response singing of the Indian kirtan combines many repetitions of a deity's name or a sacred formula with the least amount of conscious mental activity. It casts an extraordinary spell. At certain Hindu festivals, chanting will continue for eight hours or more, an experience as trance inducing and meditative as the dances of the so-called Whirling Dervishes, followers of the famous Persian mystic Rumi.

Another practice with similar power is what we might call swarming—moving and acting with a large number of fellow worshippers. How it feels to be caught up in a swarm of devotees is vividly captured in this account by Linda Johnsen, an American follower of the Indian goddess tradition:

> I hear the shouting: *"Sarasvati ki jai!"* (Victory to the Goddess of Wisdom!) Of course! I lose track of time in India . . . and I'd forgotten today is Sarasvati Puja, one of several annual holidays in which all Hindu India celebrates the Mother of the Universe. . . . Here in India, 600,000,000 Hindus pour out into the streets shouting the Mother's names. Now this is what I call a Goddess festival! *"Sarasvati—"*
>
> *"Ki jai!"* I join in the call. A young boy standing beside my taxi lifts his squirter and blasts me with red powder. It's all over my face, my hair, my dusty Punjab travel outfit. We both laugh as he flings himself back into the celebration. Colored powder is flying everywhere: the air is giddy with jubilation.
>
> Then the Goddess herself appears, clad in radiant white, playing her lute, while her extra hands clasp the book she's composed and the rosary with which she recites her own name. She is mature, beautiful, tranquil, and luminous. Beside her feet, a white swan serenely surveys the crowd. . . .
>
> Jubilant children are carrying the Mother of the Universe to the river in a palanquin strewn with flowers. . . . Everyone is laughing and hollering as the Divine Mother approaches. My driver edges our auto-rickshaw to the side of the road so she can pass by. . . . Everyone here feels her blessing energy as she is carried along the road. With incredible delight, I leap out of the auto-rickshaw to join the celebration.[6]

In a Hindu chariot festival, like the famous procession of Jaggarnath, which gives us the English word "juggernaut," the deity comes out to survey his or her domain in a chariot pulled by hundreds of devotees. Food offerings are passed around or tossed in the air, priests and onlookers shout instructions, camphor flames are offered and shared, and the god rides serenely about it all, borne on an atmosphere that mixes playfulness, devotion, danger, and awe. The experience can be overwhelming.

Without some larger structure, of course, such festivals could fall into mere riot or hooliganism. But nobody would put up with that larger structure without some release from the self of the monkey mind and its chatter. The spirit is always anarchistic, like life itself, and we sometimes need crowds of children, noise and color, and violations of propriety, like having red powder blown into our face, before we are willing to get out of our own auto-rickshaws and live in the real world.

Other religious practices are anything but explosive. Take meditation, for example. The person sitting cross-legged or in lotus position, eyes closed or unfocused, has become a visual cliché for calm and peace of mind. But meditation isn't a practice of avoidance or repression like the one caricatured in the "Serenity now" episode of the sitcom *Seinfeld*. It's an exploratory process in which we gradually learn to *allow* ourselves to become calm, and it depends in part on letting the conscious mind lapse into silence.

The beginner at insight meditation is told to sit quietly and pay attention to the rise and fall of her breath. If thoughts arise, she is told, she should note them and let them go. Just about everyone who tries this discovers at once that the task is impossible. Sitting quietly only seems to turn up the volume on our monkey mind, and instead of watching thoughts come, go, and disappear, we find ourselves falling into one train of thought after another. Our mental landscape resembles Las Vegas at night or a radio set to "scan." In no particular order, we fret over our finances, think about menus for dinner, listen to a snatch of remembered music, try to recall who we're supposed to have lunch with on Tuesday, and worry that we have no future at all as meditators and that the meditation workshop was a waste of time. We keep ignoring the breath that we're supposed to watch. We even forget that we're breathing.

Unpleasant and disconcerting as this is, it's exactly what is supposed to happen. Meditation aims at stilling the mind, but we can't do that until we discover that our minds are *not* still. We have to learn what the problem is before we can accept a solution, and few of us have any idea how much mental static we generate until we sit down to meditate. Most of the time, in fact, we're barely aware of the self-conscious mind itself. We generally live lives of near-constant distraction, where any sort of thinking slips out of consciousness; we're so busy doing things and keeping in contact and being entertained that even the constant chatter of the monkey mind is drowned out by artificially stimulated emotions and loud kinesthetic feedback. (Indeed, this may be the very reason that we're addicted to distractions.)

Sitting still induces mild sensory deprivation. This turns a spotlight on the mind's constant wheel spinning and gives us a clearer picture of our mental life than we generally get. But we also get a chance to see that there's something in us that stands apart from all the noise. I remember a conversation at Oberlin College in which a student complained that he felt miserable all the time, and a visiting Buddhist monk asked him in response, "What's the part of you that knows that you're miserable?"

The monk's point was that the student could observe his own misery and learn not to identify with it. This is not the same thing as reflecting on unhappy emotions or trying to understand them; those are just further turnings of the self-conscious mind, no matter how sophisticated their psychology, and all they do is enhance and extend the very thoughts that we're trying to let go of. Nor is it the same as ignoring or repressing feelings, which has the same effect. The aim of meditation is to move us outside those turnings altogether, towards a place where there is nothing but pure awareness. This weakens our emotional investment in the thoughts that fill our head and the things that those thoughts are about. Deprived of that added impetus, the turnings then start to slow down, and the monkey mind finds fewer and fewer things to say. We are gradually and gently freed from our self-identification with the conscious mind.

Identifying with this awareness instead of our thoughts helps cure us of a kind of mental hypochondria. People who suffer from hypochondria pure and simple don't have any more symptoms than other people; they're just more likely to overinterpret every sensation as the sign of something dreadful. This makes the symptoms loom larger, and that, of course, triggers even more worry. If the sufferer can learn to note symptoms and let them go instead of dwelling on them, the aches most often work themselves out and the sniffles vanish. Meditation can work on our emotions in the same way. We begin to see that a morning's sadness is not the sign of an onset of depression but simply an emotion that like all others will eventually pass away. The world becomes less fearsome, and as a result we become less defensive and more gentle, more open, and more compassionate.

In Glucklich's two-part formulation, sensory deprivation expands the sense of self. As the experience of meditation also shows, however, this is not the same as megalomania. If you sit still for a long time with your eyes closed, you can easily begin to lose the everyday sense of where your body ends. You're no longer getting feedback from the rub of clothing against your skin, and in an enclosed space no breeze blows across your hands and face. Your attention seems to stretch unimpeded from the center of your body out to the walls of the room and infinitely far beyond. But you don't feel that your power extends infinitely—what expands is only the space in which you live.

Like the altered consciousness of the vision quest, the unboundedness we feel in meditation happens to coincide with a neglected aspect of reality. In everyday life we're acutely aware of the surface of our skin. This is necessary for our survival. One of our most important tasks as an organism is to preserve the integrity of our bodies, so we need to know where we stop and where something else begins. Every animate being has to do this; as we saw, even amoebas move away from the prick of a needle.

Useful though this feedback is, though, it reinforces the perception that we are entirely enclosed within our bodies. We're not, of course. Organisms have to preserve themselves, but they have to do this while remaining open to the world, or else they die. The skin is permeable. We breathe in the outside as the air that fills our lungs, and we consume it as food. We traffic in smells and chemical signals from all our neighbors, and we echo and send back the gestures and feelings of the others around us. The expansive world that we sense in meditation is as much a reality as the skin-wrapped body that we're usually aware of.

The vastness we experience also puts the self-obsessed turnings of monkey mind into perspective. As a Buddhist monk told a friend of mine, "The mind is very large; there's room to dance." In that space we can let experience itself assume a different form and feel. The intricate circular mandalas found in Tibetan Buddhism are meant to fill this space and change our experience of who we are. The geometric yantras of Hinduism are similar. The interwoven triangles of the Sri Chakra, for instance, show us the forms through which the divinity unfolds into the splendor and diversity of the universe. Meditating on a mandala or yantra or murmuring the right mantra moves us toward the clarity, detachment, and bliss we see in the images of the gods. The difference between us and them is not great, after all; it is in part that they are not distracted from reality as we are.

These may seem strange or even blasphemous activities to those raised in a monotheist tradition, and mandalas and yantras may look like the products of an overactive imagination rather than diagrams of reality. The most common religious practice in the monotheistic religions, though, is also tied in with imagination. That practice is prayer.

We're so used to thinking that communication is identical with the words that go back and forth that we may think of prayer as a message and assume that its only significance is in its content. People whose practice is prayer know differently. Prayer aims at presence, not information exchange. The words of a prayer count, but their deeper task is to build a relationship with the divine. People pray because prayer beings them into the presence of their god.

The right words, spoken with the right intention, can transform an ordinary moment into a meeting with the divine. Sally Kempton explains in a magazine article,

It doesn't matter what state you're in, or even what your motive is, when you begin prayer—as long as you're willing to give it a go. "If you can't pray sincerely, offer your dry, hypocritical prayer," Rumi writes, "for God in his mercy accepts bad coin."
A student of mine . . . describes how this works. "I usually start out in a rote sort of way. But if I stick with it, there is a moment when I become intensely present in the prayer. It feels like plugging an electric cord into a socket. I can feel the energy change. There is total connectivity."[7]

Like virtue, the reward in the prayer is ultimately the prayer itself. It comes in the sense of intimacy and oneness with something more deeply real:

> Through any . . . form[] of prayer, you can move from feeling the divine as separate to feeling communion with it, to the experience of merging into the object of prayer. That is when prayer becomes a form of worshipful meditation.[8]

Prayer, then, is a way of dispelling separation. It makes manifest that union with the universe that we feel in moments of spontaneous coordination and at any other time when we are deeply present and open to all things. It does so in an unequal relationship, however. You cannot pray without humility—and you cannot escape the monkey mind without it, either. Real prayer has little to do with self-improving affirmations or reminders to oneself. It brings us face-to-face with something immensely larger than our self-conscious mind, and it encourages us to surrender the self-gratifying illusion that we are in control of our own lives. In directly emotional ways, the surrender of oneself in devotion opens up a space in which the worshipper can let her world and herself be changed.

Presence is everything, and presence is the explicit object of the Hindu *pula*. In *puja*, the deity is welcomed into a consecrated image and offered food, drink, perfume, and light before being bade farewell. It may even be bathed, dressed, fanned, and combed. The entire ritual reproduces what is expected of a good host welcoming a royal visitor. What the *puja* evokes, then, is the temporary presence of the deity and her fellowship with a humble and grateful worshipper. It uses images, offerings, hand gestures, prostrations, and all the senses instead of words alone, and there is often more of a sense of the innate connection between deity and devotee than Christians would accept, but it aims at exactly the same kind of intimacy that is the deepest form of prayer.

There's no special shape or form that religious practices have to take; in fact, a good many westerners have adopted one without realizing that this is what they've done. It's estimated that some 15 million Americans regularly practice yoga, and there is a substantial business in yoga clothing, yoga equipment, and yoga classes, workshops, and retreats. For many of these people—perhaps most of them—yoga is simply an excellent form of physical exercise. Those who practice in yoga centers instead of gyms or recreation programs usually learn more. They find that yoga, like meditation, is meant to calm the chatter of the self-conscious mind and that it gains immeasurably in depth and power when it's practiced within an Indian context. As a result, there's been increased Western interest in Hinduism, and Indian devotional practices like kirtan have become more popular and visible. For all that, however, the subtlety and depth of yoga aren't well known outside the circle of serious practitioners.

What we call "yoga" in the West is not "purely" Indian. Today's posture practice draws heavily from nineteenth-century European physical culture and women's "harmonial exercise."[9] For all the diversity of its sources, however, it found its modern form and its proper home in India as one of many "yogas." The Sanskrit term is related to the English word "yoke"—as in the equipment used to harness oxen to a cart—and to practice yoga of any sort is to allow oneself to be driven by the divine as an ox is driven by the drover.[10] But the Sanskrit word also suggests integration, and the ultimate aim of yoga is to unite the practitioner with the fundamental processes of the universe.

The Western "yoga" is closest to traditional *hatha* yoga, a system of postures and exercises that dates back thousands of years. Although it's often considered a kind of preliminary practice, suitable for beginners who don't yet have the discipline to do lengthy meditations and austerities, its reach is astonishingly broad and deep. Contrary to what many people believe, the aim of yoga is not the ability to stand in bizarre and uncomfortable positions. It is meant to turn practitioners towards the inner experience of moving and keeping still. The physical techniques slowly but inexorably open windows on our bodily experience, which is not separate from our mental life, and they dramatize and throw into relief the difference between the clear, impartial awareness of our deepest nature and the roiling, ever-changing life of the self-conscious mind. It also reveals ever more subtle and illuminating forms of bodily experience itself.

The breath is as important to yoga as posture. There is an entire discipline of breath control called *pranayama* that some practitioners eventually take up, but even the most basic yoga practice involves the breath. The first task in yoga is to learn how to breathe deeply and fully. The most common teaching is that there are three parts to the breath. The first is the abdominal breath, which spreads out the stomach area. The next is chest breath, signaled by a spreading of the rib cage, and the third and last is the thoracic breath, which lifts the collarbone. The complete three-part breath opens up the entire front of the body, ultimately spreading and relaxing the shoulders. Exhalation follows the same pattern in reverse, and a complete exhalation is achieved by drawing the navel toward the back of the spine.

It is rare for westerners to breathe this deeply and almost as rare for them to be aware of their breath at all. Singers, actors, and players of wind instruments generally have to practice for weeks or months before they can "breathe from the diaphragm." Most of us breathe from the chest only, often with our shoulders hunched together, taking in air with rapid gulps.

The differences between these two styles of breathing extend beyond the amount of oxygen that gets to the bloodstream. Chest breathing is a symptom and a product of taut muscles and generalized tension. It is the breathing of someone enclosed within a tight defensive perimeter and always on guard, ready to repel an attack. The cause-and-effect relationship can be reversed with equal force, though, because this fast, shallow breathing feeds the very state of tension that called it forth in the first place, and it never allows the body to relax. Even without any reinforcing responses from others, this cycle both fixes and perpetuates the experience of the isolated, beleaguered self that is so common in the modern world. What is more, this tension makes it hard for us to be aware of anything else in our bodies.

We all know that full, deep breathing has a calming effect. Contrary to many people's stereotype, though, yoga is not a way of making yourself calm any more than meditation is. It's a way to free up emotions so that they can subside toward tranquillity; to explore the interplay of body, mind, emotion, and action; to discover a way out of the traps that we set for ourselves; to become aware of the "subtle body" that most clearly connects us with others; and to live on good terms with the world. These are matters of embodied knowledge, not discursive knowledge. Without a short discussion of yoga theory, however, we might not understand how this practice can accomplish any of those goals.

The classical text that links today's yoga to the vast and diverse Indian philosophical tradition is a tiny book called the *Yoga Sutra*, traditionally ascribed to someone named Patanjali.[11] Scholars continue to dispute whether the author was the Patanjali who wrote a Sanskrit grammar around 200 BCE, a different person with the same name living about 400 or 500 years later, or someone else whose work was eventually assigned to one or the other historical Patanjali. In any event, the *Yoga Sutra* is a work of great age and even greater penetration, and it richly deserves the many commentaries that it has accumulated over the years. It sets out the "eight-limbed path" of yoga, a set of ethical and practical principles still followed by students, and it sketches the rewards of practice in what may or may not be hyperbole. But the heart of the *Yoga Sutra* is a brilliant analysis of the intertwining of action and experience.

Patanjali—or whoever else wrote his book—divides up experience in an unusual way. We see ourselves as minds in bodies, and for all the huge differences between the world of twenty-first-century modernity and ancient India, it seems plain that many of Patanjali's contemporaries thought along the same lines. We know this because Patanjali devoted a lot of his book to explaining that we are *not* our minds. He himself was a dualist, unlike the practitioners of tantra and the nondualist Vedanta thinkers who dominated much of Indian philosophy in later years. His is a world of subject and object. But he did not divide up the world into mind and body in the same way that Descartes did. For Patanjali and for Indian philosophy in general, almost all of the activities that we think of as mind are just extremely subtle aspects of the body. Mental operations aren't separated from matter as they are in most Western thinking. They're activities of the material world just like digestion.

Patanjali's own distinction is between the observer and the phenomenal world. The observer is the true or essential self, and it is nothing but seeing or reflexivity; as he says, "The observer is simply the subject of observing."[12] The mind, on the other hand, is part of the phenomenal world, which also encompasses all the overtly physical aspects of reality. Our downfall comes when we confuse the observer with the world and our real self with the contents of the mind—mixing up the seer with the seen.

All this is implied by the first four lines of the *Yoga Sutra*, a kind of abstract that condenses an already compact text into the smallest possible space:

This is the teaching of yoga.
Yoga is the cessation of the turnings of thought.

When thought ceases, the spirit stands in its true identity as observer
to the world.
Otherwise, the observer identifies with the turning of thought.[13]

The turnings of thought are part of the material world, and like the
body itself, they're intimately connected with everything else that
goes on in the universe. All our thoughts and actions are the activity
of the totality of things, not the expression of an individual self. The
most famous of Hindu scriptures, the *Bhagavad Gita*, is as firm as can
be imagined on this point:

All work is performed by the gunas [constituents] of Prakriti
[material nature]
His atman deluded by his ego,
Man thinks, *I am the doer.*[14]

This is very close to the picture that we have developed in the other
chapters of this book, except that for Patanjali, as for Krishna, matter
and the observer are separate.[15] The may be one reason that the *Gita*
has appealed to Christians more than any other Hindu text. Krishna
sometimes seems to stand apart from creation, just as the god of
monotheism does, and he is to be worshipped instead of being iden-
tified with. Yet Krishna's teachings are meant to show his friend
Arjuna that true liberation consists of doing what the moment
demands without attachment or ego. The result is an absolute commitment to the movement of the totality of things, to the play of
the divine.

Outside the observer there is incessant action, and actions have
consequences. The two can't be separated, and the Sanskrit word
karma, which has all but passed over into English as meaning "fate,"
in fact means "action." Patanjali was interested in the lasting effects
of action—not acts of kindness or the obvious misdeeds that we generally think of as making for "good karma" or "bad karma" but everyday actions and thoughts. He taught that these leave behind
unconscious traces that not only determine rebirths (he was an

orthodox believer in reincarnation) but also predispose us to experience the world in particular ways.

Because we attach ourselves to the world, wanting one thing rather than another and believing in the permanence of things and a substantial self, our actions leave behind predilections and tendencies that Patanjali calls *ashaya*, or "subliminal intentions." These are like seeds that bear fruit when their time comes. They remain latent until some echo of the past activates them, and then they color the ways in which the world appears to us and they direct our emotional responses. They lead us in one direction instead of others, generally by inspiring either desire or aversion. Thanks to their silent influence, certain aspects of experience become fearsome or disgusting, and others become fascinating or alluring.

Hamlet said, "There is nothing either good or bad but thinking makes it so." He was right, but he didn't go far enough. The thinking that makes things either good or bad is unconscious, and it lays down habits of judging that compel our responses to anything and everything—a hamburger, a one-night-stand, a morning at church, an afternoon yoga class, a kitten, a special project at work, a favor for a friend, a migrant worker, a flag from a foreign country, or a book on religion. Our impressions of everything seem to be immediate and objective. Patanjali would disagree. All these are shaped by subliminal intentions. We ourselves create the prejudices that make us prejudge *everything*, and we are constantly creating new ones.

This unacknowledged past dictates our present experience, and this, of course, affects what we do. These actions, in turn, lay down their own subliminal intentions, in most cases reinforcing the ones that called them forth to begin with. The patterns of fear, avoidance, and blindness that we discussed in Chapter 6 develop through this process as we layer intention after subliminal intention around a seed the way a pearl grows around a piece of grit. These are Patanjali's way of talking about the networks of memory and desire that we mentioned in connection with Dawkins's theory of memes.

But how does this psychological theory tie into yoga? The connection would be obvious if we weren't used to our own mind-body distinction. We assume that our memories, hopes, fears, and evasions are private mental events and somehow immaterial. They should have as little effect on the physical body as a software update would have on the physical structure of a computer. For Patanjali, however, our thoughts are real material events and leave material traces behind. Our subliminal impressions and intentions are aspects of our bodies. That's where we encounter them, and if we're very attentive we can feel them at work. They show up as numbness or as points of tightness, as forcing, or as holding.

Because mind and body are aspects of a unity, we can do psychology simply by learning to experience our bodily lives more fully. This is a large part of what yoga accomplishes. A good session brings as many muscles as possible into play, different groups in turn. This provides an excellent overall workout, to be sure, but it also brings attention to every place where holding or tightness might signal a subliminal intention at work. The point is not to hit a posture and move on to the next, though there is certainly a place for this, and though a flowing style of yoga can address similar issues in a different way. The aim of practice is to bring the entire body into focus, piece by piece, by relaxing at each posture into a state of open and alert attentiveness.

This work depends on a balance between activity and quiet. Different postures evoke different emotional responses and trigger different subliminal intentions. (These often bubble up spontaneously, too, since our bodies and minds are very far from being quiet, and they try to take over whatever posture we happen to be in.) Keeping the body in proper alignment makes it easier to hold the pose, and this reduces muscle strain and tension that can mask our deeper emotions and physical states. By softening, allowing our breath to deepen and loosen, and surrendering tension when we find it within ourselves, we gradually move our awareness toward the points of resistance that mark our more profound and intense wounds. Through repetition and practice, that resistance begins to weaken. The intention that blocks our way fades a bit whenever we bring it to awareness and surrender some of our defensiveness. Once that happens, the holding, too, loses some force. We may find ourselves in an emotional crisis, or we might relax into an experience that we had avoided for years, watching without judgment as waves of emotion pass through us. As we slowly soften and release the innumerable layers of holding and tension, we start to let go of our self-inflicted blindnesses and fear of experience. Experience itself becomes deeper, wider, less problematic, and more pleasurable both on and off the mat.

Most of us are enslaved to our subliminal intentions, but yoga has the power to liberate us. It helps us unlearn the habits that have kept us from reality. Through it, we can begin to see ourselves as open to the world, discovering that we are not the same as the fixed patterns of like and dislike and desire and avoidance that we once thought made up our real self. No longer dependent on them for a sense of who we are, no longer gambling on their satisfaction to give us the wherewithal for happiness, we find it easier—bit by bit—to let go of the illusions of stability and control and uncover the surprising joy that they conceal.

This is not the only way in which yoga frees us from our monkey mind. Paying attention to the body's inner state—becoming used to kinesthetic awareness and other types of knowing—gives us an object of attention outside the self-conscious mind. Better yet, we begin to see that the self-conscious mind can't help us. Its stories and theories come out of and reinforce the patterns set up by our subliminal intentions. They are not the cure; they are the disease. As we open ourselves to the wordless experience of living, we begin to surrender those, too.

Yoga helps us live within our bodies instead of our thoughts, and the life of the body is incomparably richer than any story that the inner narrator can concoct. It could hardly be otherwise, because what we sense in the subtle body that we discover through yoga is the ebb and flow of everything, fully present in the flesh. Paradoxically, our inner experience becomes far more enthralling once we let go of it. Seeing ourselves as the seer, we can now take full delight in the luminous play of the seen.

This same insight can be found in similarly dualist terms in the *Bhagavad Gita*, where Krishna says,

> This body is the Ksetra or the Field,
> Who knows it is Ksetrajna, the Knower of the Field. . . .
> The only knowledge worth knowing
> Is knowledge of the Field and of the Knower of the Field[16]

In other words, the field is the phenomenal world, and the knower of the field is the observer. Seeing this separation—understanding that the witness is the self and the mind and body are the world—is Krishna's true knowledge.

Both Patanjali's *Yoga Sutra* and the *Bhagavad Gita* are dualist. Nondualist traditions like tantra go further. The tantric schools refuse to separate the observer from the physical and mental worlds or the divine from the mundane. They teach that we are *both* the field and the knower of the field. And there is nothing so strange about this extraordinary claim if we are willing to agree that every aspect of the world, consciousness included, flows forth from a single source.

What is revealed in the body is not a bundle of biological urges or an individual's thoughts. It is the entire life of the universe, past and present. The witness in Patanjali's dualist philosophy sees one perspective on the entirety of things, and if she can experience this without grasping at it and claiming it as her own, she shares the knowledge of the gods. Krishna sees through everyone's eyes, and she has only her own, but she sees what comes before her *like* Krishna does—with absolute clarity—and she sees *as* Krishna himself because both she and the god see reality impersonally, without judgment or partiality. Both of them see by the same light. And the adept of tantra goes farther, beyond seeing, beyond the duality of subject and object and seer and seen, until she lives every moment of life as the play of the divine and knows herself to be the goddess that she and all of life truly is.

Whatever our philosophical commitment, it is only through such attentive concentration on our own embodied experience that we can free ourselves from evasions and prejudices and come to experience reality itself. Only the body is honest enough to show it to us. The different postures of yoga, the repetitions of a mantra, and the visualizations of mandala or yantra practice—all of these practices quiet our thinking so that we can hear what the body has to say.

In reality, yoga is not that different from other religious practices. What sets it apart are its open acknowledgment that the wisdom it offers is bodily wisdom and its overt reliance on moving and holding the body. In all the practices that we've glanced at, though, it's the body that takes the lead. All of them rely on the shifts in awareness and experience that happen when the body is brought to do new things, whether it is dancing or singing for hours on end, running along with thousands of others, being kept sleepless, starving, and cold; pierced by bone needles and hung from a pole; brought to a state of humble attentive expectation through prayer; or set still and allowed to settle into a state of undisturbed quiet. Every one of these practices encourages the mind to listen as the body speaks.

This is not to say that all religious traditions are ultimately identical or that all of them point to the same experience. They move in the same direction, but they do so only by transforming experience, and as long as we remain in the realm of experience—as we must if we are not to leave our humanness behind—we will find ourselves grounded in a cultural and personal past and a community's specific expectations and forms of thought. Reality is beyond the split between subject and object, but we never pass over to that side, at least not without giving up our return ticket, and on this side the most godly vision appears in the language of men and women.

No mystical vision, regardless of its depth, can thus provide more than a perspective on the totality of things, and some perspectives may well be rationally incompatible with others while still opening on the same unchartable terrain. This can't be helped. There could be one universal religious tradition only if the world were one culture (if then), and we are better off that this won't ever happen, just as Hindus are better off for the riot of different gods. Yet in spite of this variety and seeming discord, there are points on which virtually every practice seems to converge. Regardless of cultural contexts and theological explanations, the body almost always tells us that our real life is perfection itself and that it is filled with light and the deep bliss of being loved.

This seems to be the hardest truth about ourselves to bring into awareness, but it is always being discovered, everywhere. The modern Indian sage Amma said, "In this universe it is love that binds everything together," and the Catholic philosopher David Walsh writes of "the luminosity that discloses reality from within."[17] Mystics of all traditions have described union with the divine in terms that sound disturbingly erotic; they have few alternatives because we have no other vocabulary to suggests the joy that exceeds joy. The term for ultimate reality in Indian philosophy includes the lovely word *ananda*, "bliss"; the experience of existence itself is bliss. Psalm 34 says, "taste and see that the Lord is good," and one taste of reality is enough to knock you flat or set your whole body to dancing.

All this can sound like mysticism or foolishness. The world is dark and cruel, and life is harsh. Nature is "red in tooth and claw"; it has no "luminosity." How can this be a universe knit together by love? How can we rejoice in it? It is hard to resist these questions, and there may be no reason why we should. But it may be, instead, that we are looking at the identification from the wrong end. We do not discover that the universe is love. That would be just another bit of discursive knowledge. Love is the means through which we encounter the universe as it is.

The universe may or may not treat us like a lover, but when we love we live the life of the universe and not our own. To be fully present in that love can seem all but impossible. It demands great insight and absolute self-surrender. But even those of us who feel ourselves to be many lives away from enlightenment can recognize what that life would be like, and from time to time we somehow have the grace to live it. In those moments we are radiantly fearless, fully engaged with others, one with Shiva's dance which moves our limbs and our heart. We are joyously alive in love, and what is love but the willingness to embrace whatever comes? Love is not an emotion but a way of living, and we can feel the universe lit up by love because the way of being of love is none other than the universe's own way of being. Love goes beyond a cold acceptance of events because it does not try to maintain a distance from anything; it embraces all and it makes no exceptions. Beauty, ugliness, joy, horror, kisses, cruelty, murder, and devotion—love takes them all into itself. To love is simply to live wholeheartedly in the fullness of knowledge, and to live fully, without any judgment or defense against what is, is to love the universe as the universe would love itself. And that is what it does in us spontaneously whenever we allow ourselves to live as we really are, because by some strange twist of biological fate, we happen to be points at which the universe reflects on and can love itself.

Notes

1. Lame Deer, John Fire, and Richard Erdoes, *Lame Deer, seeker of visions: The life of a Sioux medicine man* (New York: Simon & Schuster, 1972), 108.
2. Peter Nabokov, *Two Leggings: The making of a Crow warrior* (Lincoln: University of Nebraska Press, 1967), 62.
3. Nabokov, *Two Leggings*, 63.
4. Nabokov, *Two Leggings*, 105–6.

5. Ariel Glucklich, *Sacred pain: Hurting the body for the sake of the soul* (Oxford: Oxford University Press, 2003), 59.

6. Linda Johnsen, *The living goddess: Reclaiming the tradition of the mother of the universe* (St. Paul, MN: Yes International, 1999), 26–29.

7. http://www.sallykempton.com/resources/articles/answer-to-your-prayers (original in *Yoga Journal*).

8. http://www.sallykempton.com/resources/articles/answer-to-your -prayers (original in *Yoga Journal*).

9. See Mark Singleton, *Yoga body: The origins of modern posture practice* (Oxford: Oxford University Press, 2010).

10. In this sense, "yoga" is much like the Arabic "Islam," which means "submission"; in both yoga and Islam, the devotee surrenders herself to someone or something else.

11. There are a great many translations and commentaries on this text, some of them very far removed from the intellectual world of the original. All citations to the *Yoga sutras* in this book are to Barbara Stoller Miller, trans., *Yoga: Discipline of freedom: The* Yoga Sutra *attributed to Patanjali* (Berkeley: University of California Press, 1996).

12. Miller, *Yoga*, 49: II:20.

13. Miller, *Yoga*, 29: I:1–4.

14. P. Lal, trans., *The Mahabharata of Vyasa: The complete Bhishma parva* (Kolkata: Writers' Workshop Press, 2006), 143; VI:27:27. Conventionally, Bhagavad Gita II:27. Reprinted with permission.

15. Vyasa is the traditional author of the *Mahabharata*, in which the *Gita* is found.

16. *The Mahabharata of Vyasa*, 243: VI:37:2–3. Conventionally, Bhagavad Gita 13:2–3.

17. Walsh, David. *The modern philosophical revolution: The luminosity of existence* (Cambridge; Cambridge University Press, 2008), 11.

9

Both Perfect and Broken

But it is time now to return to earth, to the science-religion debate with which we started, and to the indictment drawn up by the new atheists. So let us review their allegations. They charge religion with a number of specific crimes, as most criminal indictments do, too, and three in particular stand out. The first is that religion is a "bad thing," leading us toward irrational violence and hatred where science encourages rational thinking and tolerance. Next is the charge that religions consist of false explanations of phenomena that science explains correctly. Third and last is that religions coddle us with comforting illusions and encourage us to indulge in wishful thinking in contrast to the hardheaded attachment to reality cultivated by science. All these allegations are related, of course, but then so are most of the counts in any criminal indictment, and like any criminal jury, we're still entitled to consider each of them in turn.

The bad-thing argument has already been discussed, I hope adequately. There's no doubt that religious notions and classifications have been invoked by the perpetrators of terrible slaughter, but so have nonreligious ideas and categories. Religion is a handy excuse, but the sources of our species' nastiness and brutality lie elsewhere—in the delusions of self-consciousness, our hardwired self-centeredness, the psychological and spiritual toll of living in hierarchical and unequal societies, and the stony failure of life to fulfill our hopes and expectations. Take religion away, and human violence would still be with us. The atheists' cure is a pipe dream.

In fact, few religious ideas are any more delusional than the insistence that the world would be a peaceable place if only people followed reason instead of emotion. This is a fantasy out of *Star Trek*, not a serious solution for our problems. We are not rational creatures. Nothing we can do or say will make us any different. In the words of the philosopher David Hume, "Reason is, and ought only to be the slave of the passions."[1] As useful as it can be when we want to know how to do something, rationality is all but useless when we need to decide *what* to do. It does not allow us to set goals, chart a path to a satisfying life, or even figure out what model car to buy. For all these, we have to rely on our emotions. Without feelings we find ourselves adrift.

What's more, the reasons we come up with to explain our choices—emotional, rational, or religious—turn out to be rationalizations, not the motivators that we think they are. They are little more than pleasant stories about ourselves, fairy tales from the imagined realm where we are ideal agents effortlessly formulating and carrying out our plans. The roots of our actions are rarely the same as our monkey-mind fables about ourselves. Turning the human race into Mr. Spocks would be a failure on several different levels, then; we couldn't become rational beings, rational beings are no good at the business of life, and rationality operates at too superficial a level to do much good anyway. Not only is religion not the villain here; science and reason are not going to be our saviors.

The next count of the indictment is that religion is, in effect, bad science, telling us things about the universe that simply aren't so. This is often true, of course. The new atheists have no trouble showing us that adherents of every religious tradition frequently spout nonsense. Literal interpretations of the first chapter of Genesis are the targets closest to hand, but anyone can produce a similar list, and anyone with even a small amount of intellectual honesty can do it out of his or her own tradition alone.[2]

There's no point, though, in complaining that religious explanations are wrong. *All* explanations are wrong if you expect them to give you ultimate, absolute truth. Simply put, every discussion requires a starting point, and these starting points can never be justified.[3] All we can hope for in a starting point is that it invites everyone to the conversation and that it allows the most far-ranging discussions. Being open is more important than being right. Unlike being absolutely and truly right, openness to some degree or other is at least possible.

This is not to say that there's no such thing as reality. There is. It's not a mere social or cultural convention, something that we make up or agree on. But *descriptions* of reality are indeed social and cultural conventions. They're always inadequate, period, because they start by cutting reality in two—into subject and object. That's one reason that all of them have to start from arbitrary assertions. And science is not exempt from this rule. As Immanuel Kant demonstrated in the 1780s, science is coherent, reliable, and lawlike, but it is a coherent, reliable, and lawlike account of how things appear to us, not how they are in themselves.

There can be no hope that new equipment, supercolliders, space telescopes, and whatnot will nail down reality as it is. All these can do is help us describe with greater and greater delicacy and accuracy how the universe appears to an "outside" observer. But the observer isn't actually outside the universe that she's trying to describe. Her results are always partial because everything that she comes up with depends on the betrayal of reality—the sundering of the unity of observer and observed. Reality vanishes the moment she takes her first step.

In the physical sciences this problem can generally be left to one side. All we need are reliable predictions about appearances. If we hope to learn anything about what we really are, though, the separation between observer and observed—between subject and object—creates all kinds of trouble. That's why the "human sciences" will never resemble the physical ones. Limiting ourselves to appearances leaves us in a dilemma. We appear to ourselves as human machines who have thoughts and experiences we can't explain on the one hand or as conscious ghosts in charge of robotic bodies on the other. Neither picture can be true, but as scientists of the human we have no alternatives.

Many scientists and philosophers insist that there is no problem, that mental events are identical with brain activity. But this is not a solution. It just denies that the problem exists and ignores the abyss between patterns of neuron activity and subjective experience.[4] Many thoughtful scientists have some sense of this, but it doesn't look like the same insight plays a part in the new atheists' thinking. All seem to share the unfounded and hubristic belief that the methods of physics can solve the problems of philosophy and religion—that they can tell us who and what we are and how we should live our lives.

This failing doesn't just cripple their understanding of religion. It throws a monkey wrench into their picture of science and their faith that they can arrive at a science of humanity. Sam Harris, for instance, thinks that neuroscience can even support a universal code of ethics, something that all the world's philosophers have failed to produce despite centuries of trying.[5] This position has none of the modesty of genuine scientific inquiry. It is not science but "scientism," the belief that science can answer all the questions of life. In one sense, then, there is no big-time debate between science and religion. It's a debate between scientism on one side and the dogmatic aspects of religion on the other.

Unlike real science, scientism cannot investigate or critique its own assumptions. The atheists don't realize that they can offer only images of the real, expressed in language, symbols, theories, and formulas, and they cannot seriously allow that these might be inadequate to capture reality. Without this understanding, their position is just an especially vicious and hermetic kind of delusion. As the philosopher Ludwig Wittgenstein put it in 1918,

The whole modern conception of the world is founded on the illusion that the so-called laws of nature are the explanations of natural phenomena.

Thus people today stop at the laws of nature, treating them as something inviolable, just as God and Fate were treated in past ages. And in fact both are right and both wrong: though the view of the ancients is clearer in so far as they have a clear and acknowledged terminus, while the modern system tries to make it look as if everything were explained.[6]

The world's spiritual traditions, at their most profound, acknowledge what the atheists refuse to see. They do indeed trade in explanations, but they also always lead their adherents to go beyond those explanations to the reality that defies description. And this is not a matter of cherry-picking or explaining away inconvenient parts of a tradition that we're drawn to but can't justify. It's an integral part of the self-understanding of those traditions. It is even found in some of the very explanations that attract the atheists' scorn.

Picasso once said that art is a lie that make us realize truth.[7] This is not such a bad definition of religion, either, especially if we take his words seriously; to realize something is different from being told something.[8] Religion, like art, is not simply a way of imparting certain lessons in a particularly enticing or convincing manner. It is meant to show us what cannot be told, to bring us to different ways of using our senses, to open up a different context for the theories and stories that we take for the truth of our existence, and to change our lives by attuning us to the very different forms of experience that we inhabit when this happens.[9] Taken literally, religious claims can provide comfort and social peace at least as often as they do the opposite. Taken thoughtfully, they do something else. They set us on the path to the real and then give us a kick in the pants to send us where words cannot go. They do indeed help us *realize* the truth.

It's not that the explanations don't count. When the Buddha said that his teachings were like a raft, to be discarded after crossing the stream, he did not mean that they were to be discarded before we get to the water. Religions want us to see behind their words, but they choose those words carefully; it makes a real difference which words we happen to be looking behind. Theirs are meaningful to the extent that they grow out of, image forth, and are perpetually questioned by the life of religious practice. When that happens, they give us fruitful metaphors and images of what reality is really like. The finger pointing to the moon is not the moon, but it does point in the right direction.

But there is yet another reason for most religions' focus on explanations. Religion has rarely been a strictly private matter. For most if not all of human history, it's had social and cultural functions, too. The unprovable starting points are necessary; all communities need common points around which their members can orient themselves in their everyday lives. These have long come out of spiritual practice. The images of the human subject that even we today rely on when we imagine our places and paths through life have religious roots. When people have to think or feel their way through deep crises, when they struggle to integrate suffering into a life that retains a sense of wholeness, there is little but religious metaphor to draw on. Religions give communities the vocabulary for that work just as they frame discussions of individual and social purpose and of the nature of the good. Spiritual practice nurtures the seeds from which cultures grow and flower.

The Romans supposed that the Latin word *religio* derived from words meaning "to bind together again." Their etymology was historically wrong, but sociologically it holds up. Historically, most communities are brought together through spiritual practice and the rites, myths, metaphors, and assumptions that grow out of it. As the clear ties between the secular Western self and the self of Christianity suggest, this is true whether the members of those cultures accept religious claims or not.

For this reason above all, spiritual traditions have learned to speak to many different human conditions. As Paul did, they had to become all things to all people. In every community there will be many people who are too busy, too limited by their circumstances, or simply too prosaic in their outlook to want or need anything but simple messages of encouragement and flat assertions of fact. That is their entry into the conversation. It may be that they never stray far from their point of beginning. Just by being part of that conversation, though, there is at least the chance that they will move beyond it.

So the second charge should be dismissed. Religious explanations cannot claim to communicate the truth, but they ground the broadest and deepest discussions of the social world. They are also uniquely valuable despite and even because of their own falsity because at their best they embody and make use of the inadequacy of explanation itself. They tell us one thing and show us how to pass through those very words toward the truthfulness that no explanations can grasp.

It's largely because they have no sense that reality evades their tools that the new atheists can write off religion as mere escapism. In this third count of the indictment, though, they find unexpected allies. One common theory among those who want to carve out a space for religious life is that people have a deep need for transcendence. Put bluntly, we want wholeness in a broken world—something more than the muddled, painful, difficult, and frequently cruel life through which we slowly age and die. That's what we find in the divine.

The need for transcendence is a plausible one. But it doesn't really do anything to justify religion unless you're the kind of extreme pragmatist who cares nothing about truth and can live happily with useful and uplifting fables. Viewed coldly, the urge to transcendence is indeed awfully hard to tell apart from escapism. It assumes that religions really do just offer us pie in the sky but explains that we simply have to believe in that pie so we can get through the day.

What flowers in spiritual and religious practice, though, isn't a need for transcendence. It's a need for reality. Not everybody shares this or is even aware of it, but in every place and time there have been people who can't shake off the feeling that the everyday world and everyday experience are somehow false. Self-consciousness is an all-encompassing, highly persuasive delusion, but it has cracks in its shell. For those with an eye for those cracks, the limited, skin-encased life in which we're at arms' length from everyone and every-thing else somehow doesn't seem real. The ways in which we know ourselves and deal with one another seem farcical or at least oddly askew. It all feels like a mistake.

This kind of existential breakdown wasn't a twentieth-century dis-covery. It's what has always led people to look behind the assump-tions of their particular way of life. Through the cracks in the everyday world shines light from something that all bodies of doc-trine, theology, and religious poetry try to reveal. Transformative practices like meditation, mantra recitation, yoga, and prayer all take us beyond the daylight world toward that even more dazzling light, which, for all its elusiveness, has more of the taste of reality to it. It is a taste at once familiar and strange, delicious and unsettling, euphoric and terrifying.

At the root of religious life is the deeply disconcerting light of real-ity itself. And reality *is* disconcerting. Instead of comforting and reassuring us, spiritual experience turns everything upside down and leaves us no place at all to stand. Reality does not take us by the hand and lead us into pastures of emotional plenty. It shakes us to our bones. It overwhelms and destroys, bringing not peace but a sword. The only reason to seek it out is that nothing else rings true.

In the monotheistic worldview this shock is usually connected with the sense of sinfulness, and it is often depicted as "a consuming fire"[10] that burns through all our human frailties. The association is an old one, though, long predating Christian guilt. The Greeks told stories about Zeus's human lover Semele, who asked to see the god as he really was. Bound by an oath, he complied—and she was instantly turned to ash. The early philosopher Heraclitus said it more impersonally; the universe was nothing other than a perpetual fire, he taught, blazing up and dying down in turns.[11]

There is a profound truth behind these potent images. Reality does indeed stand opposed to the everyday world. It has no place for the self that we cultivate, cherish, and protect. It mocks our every wish and every boast. Reason is a child's game, knowledge is an illusion, pleasure is a trap unless you let it come and go as it pleases, and accomplishments are mere egotism, the desperate scheming of an imaginary self to maintain its perpetually threatened stability. Death cannot be bought off. All that we hold dear crumbles like ash.

This is not a matter of the individual's being infinitesimally small and powerless in the greater scheme of things. It is because reality cannot abide the titanic self-assertion, the vast lie, of the independent self. This is the very barrier that keeps us from reality, the most dangerous of delusions. The separation of self and world is the foundation of everything that we call knowledge, yet it is fundamentally false. Sinful or pure, we cannot stand in reality unless we leave off thinking that reality is somehow "out there" to be seen, grasped, understood, or known. That means letting go of the deep-seated idea that life can be an object of our thoughts. In the end it means letting go of the thinker, too. The consuming fire of reality must burn through all divisions and separations, obliterating all the barriers that self-consciousness puts up between self and world. It leaves us not even the tiniest foothold. Jesus said, "Whosoever will save his life shall lose it: and whosoever will lose his life for my sake shall find it."[12]

To stand in reality is to die to oneself and to one's place in the conventional world. This is a shocking experience, most of all because we're rarely aware that we do place ourselves in a specific relation to reality. But we do, and the best way of understanding this is to think, for a moment, of the technique of single-point perspective that has dominated Western art since the Renaissance.[13]

We're all familiar with the rules of perspective. Objects seem to point behind the picture plane. Their lines lead us to the vanishing point, an imaginary location that stands behind the picture plane just as the viewer stands in front of it. The illusion of reality depends on the illusion that there is a world behind the canvas. The painting, then, does not appear to us as a painting, a flat surface covered with colors. It seems to be an image, a fictitious window through which we see the reality that lies behind it.

This is very much the way that we see and experience life and very much the way that conventional theism portrays it. We seem to stand apart from the world, eager or even desperate to make sense of it. And as soon we place ourselves in that spot, there seems to be a reality that produces or explains what we see. We know there's something missing, but we don't recognize that we're responsible for this loss. We've eliminated the reality of the experience by separating ourselves from it. So we imagine that there's a *real* reality, something hidden behind experience, much like we project the vanishing point behind the painting.

There is nothing unreal about the world or about ourselves, though. The cracks in the world of self-consciousness are not defects of reality. They're points where the illusion of separation breaks down—where we no longer imagine that there's another more real kind of reality or that we're apart from the real. Put another way, the appearances are not an illusion. The illusion is the belief that they are appearances of something else. This lasts only as long as we think we're separated from them. As long as that belief persists, though, we're stuck with the nagging sense that reality is somewhere else.

To encounter reality is not to pass through the illusionary world of appearances and discover the really real that hides behind it. It is to leave behind the illusion that we can stand or ever have stood apart from the real, the illusion that we can never shake as long as we cling to the self. This is so profoundly threatening that most of us run away from it, and there's no more common way to do this than to embrace the imagined real point behind experience and call it god.

The illusion of self and the illusions of conventional religion are identical, and they depend on each other.

It has been said, uncharitably but truthfully, that the main business of religion is to protect us from genuine religious experience. Yet in spite of the burden of theories, theologies, theisms, and rules, the truth of life smolders in every spiritual tradition. At the right moment, it can still blaze up and light the path for those who catch a glimpse of its radiance. Then we see appearances for what they are, as the fire of reality itself.

We know at least this much: to live fully and openly ought to be possible. Reality is not beyond us, and we are not apart from it. We are whole; we merely think ourselves into brokenness out of fear and misplaced desire. When we let the body teach the mind, then, we're letting the fragments of our broken ways of seeing and feeling come together and heal themselves. We begin to recognize ourselves and our lives as full and undivided. It's all the same life, after all, whether it comes to us in thinking, feeling, or acting, and that life flows together with all of life everywhere. There is where we feel reality in the flesh: in the dance from which subject and object both emerge—a dance in which we are both the choreographer and the dance company, bodying forth the incomprehensible life that lives and breathes in each of us and through and in between all of us. The universe is not a puppet show. To live is not to step obediently to the tune of a cosmic choreographer who charts our every move. It is to share in the creative and destructive ecstasy of the gods themselves.

This strays very little from what biology seems to be showing us, and it fits surprisingly well with a deeply religious attitude.[14] The Shavite tantrism of Kashmir teaches it this way: everyone and everything is the god Shiva, because the dance of life is his own self-concealment and self-recognition. Our lives are moments in his life, and his life is ours; we are not apart from the divine. We are liberated when we recognize this fact, the way a woman welcomes a stranger and then, in an instant of illumination and love, recognizes her long-missing husband. Put less poetically, the moment of insight is the recognition of our real biological nature as active, creative, free moments in an infinite interplay of intention and experience.

A biological view of the shape of reality is even compatible with a belief in an overall intentionality or direction to the universe. We have no real idea how deeply we are tied together, after all, or what kinds of purpose might emerge within a fully interwoven world. The intentionality of a single individual would make no sense from the perspective of a single cell, and it is not beyond reason to think that the purposefulness of the whole of things is equally invisible to us as individuals. But there is no way to answer this question. It can only be raised and not answered.

There is one question that we can answer from this perspective, though. Obliterating the separation between subject and object and between self and world gives us a foundation for a genuinely ethical life. In fact, the concrete claims that come out of spiritual practice seems necessary to ground any moral theory that is not merely arbitrary in its roots. It's not that you cannot be good without God. You can certainly live a meaningful and ethical life without any religious commitment whatsoever. But it is surprisingly hard to find any way of justifying or grounding your ethical choices without turning, at the very least, to a view of the interconnection of all things such as the one outlined here.

There is no obvious way to justify the special status we give to human beings, for example,[15] and no coherent way to assign individual responsibility for our acts. You might argue that we simply couldn't feel human unless we took responsibility for our actions. This is all but certainly true, yet that sense of responsibility is pretty dubious, universal though it is. It rests on the conviction that we have free will, and that conviction has little or no scientific or philosophical justification. The new atheists are mostly determinists, and from their perspective there is no other consistent position. Yet a strict determinism leaves no room for individual responsibility or moral choice. If you have no real power over your decisions, morality is meaningless.

Christian theologians teach that we, alone among animals, have the spirit of God within us and have been endowed with free will. We have unique value as individuals, and we have the unique ability to live up to our ethical obligations. Out of this comes the individualist, rights-based morality that's prevalent in the West.[16] Whether that kind of ethics can be justified in the absence of Christian belief is another matter. The odds are against it; both the purported special qualities of human beings and our individual freedom of action seem to be myths. Trying to ground this kind of ethical approach seems like a search for secular answers to religious questions.

Set that aside for a moment, for there are other questions to consider. Why should people be good, anyway? What's in it for them? Being good clearly doesn't have any correlation with worldly success. It doesn't have much correlation with ordinary happiness, either. This, too, is a problem that pure rationalism gets stuck at. There seems to be no reason at all to look after anyone but oneself and to pursue anyone else's happiness at the expense of one's own. From most perspectives—rational ones, at least—morality is a losing proposition. Richard Dawkins is most eloquent about acts of self-sacrifice and moral beauty, and even though he can't account for them within his own theories, he obviously thinks that these make life better. But why should we want to make life better? And what constitutes a better life?

Christianity, of course, "solves" this second problem with an afterlife of rewards and punishments. This strategy is hardly unique to Christianity, but it's both unacceptable and ultimately immoral. It's an appeal to blatant egotism and self-interest; those who make it are just as focused on themselves as the most egregious sinner. They simply figure that a heavenly distribution of pains and pleasures will trump the earthly one. Treasure in heaven is a much better investment than treasure on earth, and the point is not to be good but to be good prudent investors. Think of Pascal's wager:

> "God is, or He is not." But to which side shall we incline? Reason can decide nothing here. There is an infinite chaos which separated us. A game is being played at the extremity of this infinite distance where heads or tails will turn up.... Which will you choose then? Let us see. Since you must choose, let us see which interests you least. You have two things to lose, the true and the good; and two things to stake, your reason and your will, your knowledge and your happiness; and your nature has two things to shun, error and misery. Your reason is no more shocked in choosing one rather than the other, since you must of necessity choose.... But your happiness? Let us weigh the gain and the loss in wagering that God is.... If you gain, you gain all; if you lose, you lose nothing. Wager, then, without hesitation that He is.[17]

This is unpersuasive as well as demeaning, rewarding the hypocrite and damning the honest doubter. Worse yet, it builds morality on sand, because once the possibility of believing in a just judge vanishes, there is no restraint at all on our actions. If you are good only because God will reward you and if you conclude that God and his rewards and punishments do not exist, then everything would seem to be permitted.[18]

There's another reason for living ethically, though, that is more deeply and genuinely planted in the world disclosed in spiritual practice. It is that selflessness and humility are the doors that open onto the real. To move beyond the subject/object divide and live in the real world is to leave behind the self and all the longing for special treatment that having a self entails. You cannot get there as long as you hold on to the self, and once you let the self go, you lose all the incentives to all the sins, from the seven deadly ones on down.

We should be good, then, because living in reality is better and even more useful than living in illusion and because being truly good and living beyond illusion are one and the same thing. And the identity of selflessness, morality, and clear perception also answers other vexing questions about morality. It shows us what is truly special about being self-conscious, it shows us that we are indeed free, and it shows us what the freedom really means and consists of.

Intentionality and knowledge are present in the whole of existence, and self-consciousness is their flowering into awareness. The goddess of Hinduism claims that she is the illusion and that which dispels illusion. In the same way, self-consciousness is a trap but not merely a trap; it is also the vehicle through which the process of the whole has come to see itself. That is why self-consciousness is uniquely valuable and why we as self-conscious beings are uniquely important. It is because we are the place where the embodied knowingness of the whole of things becomes explicit.

All beings know, but only we humans know that we know. And what we know is not the inner world of a specific individual. When we understand ourselves aright, we find that we know the life of the universe itself, refracted through the specific life that each of us happens to be living. Nor is human freedom an illusion. We are free whenever we act on behalf of all beings and thus as active participants in the life of the whole. We don't control our own lives, but we all share control of the life we live together. We are not free as individuals, but we are not individuals anyway. Each of us lives one facet of the life of the universe, which itself is free and unconstrained. We are all collectively free and collectively responsible.

Self-consciousness is essential to that responsibility. It gives us at least one unique power: the power to still ourselves and wait. This is what allows us to choose between a life of immediate responses to immediate needs and one that reflects and carries forward the life of the whole. Because we have that choice, we are responsible for our acts in a way that hawks and mountain lions are not.

But self-consciousness can only set us on the right path. We cannot enter the promised land of unclouded perception and right action through it. We need it to set off, but we need to leave it aside. In the same way, we need religious teachings and masters and we need to leave them behind. They are like the spells and amulets that the heroine of a quest receives from the wise ones she encounters along the way. They direct her toward her goals and help her win through to reality, but the nature of reality is something she must discover for herself. She never knows what the gifts are really for until she uses them.

It is the same with the ethics that emerge from spiritual practice. These commit us to building a world that we cannot plan, pin down, or formulate in advance. Surprisingly, perhaps, this view of life leads us to a revolutionary politics that is far more sweeping in its demands than anything imagined by most revolutionaries. That is why spiritual practice has nurtured some of the greatest movements for social change. When it wipes away the separation between self and other, the light of reality destroys every hierarchy and system that sees people as unequal. As a Catholic scholar of Kashmir Shaivism writes,

> The same Un-namable is present with its unimaginable light, might, and pulsation in the leaders and the lost, in the rich and the lowliest, in men and women. In children, in Dalits, tribals, in the most successful and in outsiders, in plants, animals, rocks, a drop of water, a star.[19]

The life of a spiritual community, then, is a constant conversation with no goal defined in advance. This is true of any heart-to-heart that you have with a friend or lover. If you insist on ending up with a particular result, you can't have a real conversation. What counts is the openness to transformation, and both partners have to be equally open to that. And why shouldn't our public world be open in the same way?[20]

As utopian or mystical as this might sound, it is no different from the biology that we have looked at. The flow of coordination and mirroring that is the real ground of our experience is shut down wherever there is pain, terror, domination, control, or manipulation. Its movement does not stop as it encounters these barriers, but the back-and-forth drawing together of genuine community is arrested. At that point our own openness is blocked, and our own delight cannot be complete. The logic of that movement itself and the responsibility that we bear toward all the world calls on us to free everyone to join in the dance. We are neither truly free nor truly human until all creatures are free.

Here, then, religion and politics meet. Their union does not lead us to a theocratic state, where revealed religious truth is supposed to control everything everyone does or even thinks. This all-too-common horror is just another way in which religions keep us away from real religious life, yet another trick of the self-conscious mind, doomed to a self-imposed distance from reality and an irresistible tendency to force life into predetermined patterns. A genuinely spiritual political practice is different. It means surrendering our ideas about how the world should work and allowing it to shape itself through the thoughts and lives of every being alive. It means taking equality seriously and building a community in which that equality is something real and not merely juridical. It demands of us that we strive for a world in which everyone has a decent livelihood, the resources, and the time to grow, flourish, and contribute to an ever-broadening conversation made of words and deeds. We have no right to silence anyone else, even indirectly, or to speak for anyone else's experience, and we cannot acquiesce in any world in which that takes place.

Merely having free elections does nothing. In most of today's world, vast inequalities of wealth and social power give a few people a commanding voice, and everyone else's desires and thoughts are lost. Our fundamental equality is honored in theory but ignored in practice. We have built a broken world, one plagued by physical violence; the constant slow violence of poverty; the waste and oppression and soul-destroying character of most work and the waste, oppression, and soul-destroying lack of work; and racial, sexual, ethnic, and, yes, religious triumphalism and persecution—and much more.

And actual oppression is not the only way that voices are silenced. The human community seems to have been superseded by a conglomeration of atomized consumers and closeted addicts of Internet pornography or mere Internet triviality. Even those with the wherewithal to speak and act in public find that there is little that they can say now that advertising, focus-grouped public relations campaigns, and the pseudoevents of symbolic spectacle have taken over the sphere of public discourse.

This is not a new complaint, but the problem is rarely seen in the context of religion. Yet it turns out to be deeply connected with the nature of our religious life and with the changes that religion has undergone in the West. In the mid-1600s, religion was separated out from public life in most of northern Europe and made into a matter of individual conscience. This was the price of social peace. Endless religious war had convinced Protestants, at least, that combining state power and religious authority ended up harming both; self-righteous rulers became tyrants, and worldly power corrupted the churches. But the cost was a high one. Once religion became a private matter there was no public activity left that recognized and opened people up toward the seamless unity of the social world, the fundamental equality of all those who make it up, and the greater unity behind and beyond the purely human. We lost our common starting points.

Nationalism, a nineteenth-century substitute, lacked the genuine egalitarianism of religious vision, and it was founded on an obvious illusion; the special qualities of Spaniards, Americans, or Germans were generally imaginary. It turned out to be a cure that was worse than the disease. So, too, did communism. The faith in democracy is more benign, but the whole point of liberal democracy is to leave people free to frame their own ideas of the good life. As a result, the only social goal it allows is the elimination of social goals.[21]

Our many contemporary crises and the stalemates that plague almost every elected government testify to the loss of something essential. The most profound discussions and the deepest connections among people have always been forged through the practices that we call religious or spiritual. There can be no healthy and genuinely public life that is not founded on unifying and illuminating practices that are equally profound. We need shared starting points that offer the same range and the same depth as the ones we have rejected. We have none.

This is not to argue for a new constitution based on Christian principles or any sort of established religion. Instead, spirituality and political life must merge again without letting one dominate the other. Until we do that, the real world will appear to us only through the distortions of a privatized, interior religion, and our common life will remain empty of anything truly common. Our public sphere will remain what it is today, little more than a stock exchange of ideas and feelings where everyone is presumed to want only his or her own interests and where acting for any other motive is suspect or even banned. This is surely one reason for our terrifying inability to make the common sacrifices demanded by global warming and global inequality.

The "society of the spectacle" diagnosed by Guy Debord is an inevitable product not simply of capitalism. It reflects the banishment from public life of the very practices and discourses that directed people to their hidden roots and its replacement by the fraudulent commonality of consumers, viewers, and Web surfers. If we are to escape from this trap, our world must once again open itself to the shapes of reality disclosed by spiritual practice. This is a more daunting task than any other, and how it can be carried out without the utter collapse of our present way of life is hard to see. All that seems humane and compassionate is to nurture the longing for a life shared at the deepest levels and to learn to live well in its absence. But the task is there, and it cannot be avoided.

And yet even the creation of a true public world is not enough. The destruction of the public world also brought about the modern self, with its treasured independence and the accompanying fear—or even conviction—that we are isolated and alone in an alien world. This, too, must be surrendered because it is manifestly false, yet we would not—and should not—surrender the centrality of individual dignity that is one positive aspect of the modern world. We must transform ourselves in the very acts that will transform our world, so that both self and world are freed together. It could hardly be otherwise, because these two are one.

The experience of reality puts our whole life under judgment. We cannot stop here, though, because that experience itself is also under judgment. It tells us that the world is perfect just as it is—and it is all too clearly imperfect, even horrible. Darwin could never accept the liberal Christian idea that God created the world through natural selection. No benevolent deity, he said, could countenance the suffering of so many animals.[22] Leave aside the tangles that you weave the moment you think of the world as something made by an external creator, and you still find yourself stuck with a world that is exactly what it must be and is absolutely unjustifiable at the same time.

It is more than a poetic metaphor to say that we live in a middle state, both divine and brutal, heavenly and hellish. The world is both perfect and broken. So are we. And the Fall is no mere fantasy, no specious explanation for the difficulties of life. We all live in obligatory exile from our own real nature. If we think of the divine as one way of talking about the unity-beyond-unity from and in which our world is constantly unfolding, though, we need to amend the story a little bit. If the truth of our nature is that we are all moments in that unfolding, it is not humanity that has fallen but god himself.

The calling of both spiritual life and of truly emancipatory politics is to undo that fall and realize the oneness of reality. Neither of them can succeed without undoing creation itself, though. Reality cannot be inhabited as it is, and if it can be imagined, it appears as an impossibility like the Hindu figure of the Ardhanarishwara, half male and half female, Shiva on one side and Shakti on the other. The half-truths and self-made limits of the subject-object world are essential. Without them there would be nothing at all; they are necessary delusions, how the process of the whole has to be if it is to see itself at all. This is the inherent tragedy and absurdity of self-consciousness, an unsolvable dilemma that among humans too often finds expression in a rage for destruction. We are truly ourselves only when we no longer exist as selves—but then we do not exist at all.

R. H. Blyth longed for a religion that would combine the Buddha in eternal bliss and Christ in eternal agony. Yet over and against his deeply human wish, we can put the wisdom of the saints and sages, who tell us from hard-won experience that the division and oneness are identical and that suffering, however great, is unreal in the light of the still and silent joyfulness that ceaselessly and in the same moment gives birth to and receives all things. Once the shock of reality passes, the world is filled with an inexpressible lightness. We thought we were cut off from the truth, living in an illusory world of appearances, but we now see that the appearances *are* the truth. Reality is fully present everywhere. The only illusion is that there is a deity behind appearances or an observer in front of them. To know this is to pass beyond all separation and to recognize oneself and everything as entirely divine.

Our goal is unreachable because we have always been where we long to be. The philosopher Hegel once told his classes, in essence, that the only thing that keeps us from seeing the world as the full expression of Absolute Spirit is our belief that this has yet to be accomplished.[23] We cannot be free of that mistaken belief, but it no longer binds us when we open and move toward liberation, our own and that of all beings. In those acts we are one with the inner movement of all things, and we walk in the truth. Each moment in which we move that way we are already living in the richer, wider, and deeper world that is our reality both in the spirit and in the flesh. In each step we are lost and saved, unenlightened and enlightened, fully human and fully divine. We have never been anything else.

The great Buddhist sage Nagarjuna taught, in lines as deep as they are paradoxical, that no difference exists between the everyday world and Nirvana or between Nirvana and the everyday world.[24] The eighteenth-century philosopher Johann Gottlieb Fichte expressed a similar vision in the ecstatic close of his book *The Vocation of Man*:

> Thy Life, as alone the finite mind can conceive it, is self-forming, self-manifesting Will:—this Life, clothed to the eye of the mortal with manifold sensible forms, flows forth through me, and throughout the immeasurable universe of Nature. Here it streams as self-creating and self-forming matter through my veins and muscles, and pours out its abundance into the tree, the plant, the grass. Creative life flows forth in one continuous stream, drop on drop, through all forms and into all places where my eye can follow it; it reveals itself to me, in a different shape in each various corner of the universe, as the same power by which in secret darkness my own frame was formed. There, in free play, it leaps and dances as spontaneous activity in the animal, and manifests itself in each new form as a new, peculiar, self-subsisting world:—the same power which, invisibly to me, moves and animates my own frame. Everything that lives and moves follows this universal impulse, this one principle of all motion, which, from one end of the universe to the other, guides the harmonious movement;—in the animal without freedom; in me, from whom in the visible world the motion proceeds although it has not its source in me, with freedom.[25]

We may or may not find this convincing in theory, but it is undeniably true in practice. Tasting reality—really, fully, deeply, madly, lovingly, selflessly, recklessly, and openly—wipes away all fear and all pain. Unbearable as it may seem, the only thing to do with horror and pain is to embrace them. Love is the only way to live; anything else, however rational or emotionally right, leaves us outside the real and apart from our true being. It is the hardest lesson, the most difficult to swallow, but there is no other lesson to learn.

There is everything to do, then, but nothing to achieve. The world must be made over utterly, but only so we can see it as it is and has always been, something unforgivable and divine at once. Look again at Shiva dancing—Shiva nataraja. It is an image of explosive energy, yet it is totally still. Creation and destruction, death and life, are perfectly balanced. All the contradictions and contrarieties of life, all its unnecessary and necessary and unbearable pain, all its cruelty and love, everything is fully present and preserved and completely transcended, all at the same time. Shiva's right foot stands on the body of a dwarf, the puny and broken life of the self-conscious ego in which we have sought security and identity for so long, and he looks at us with compassion as he gestures to his left foot, raised in dance. Take refuge here, he tells us: in the play of all things with all things, in the movement that opens us to the unreality of the life that we think we have and the unimaginable life that is really ours. Take refuge in the dance itself. There is not and never has been anything but that dance.

This is also the vision of contemporary biology—what it can suggest but not what it can bring us into. For there is no conflict between science and religion, not if we understand them correctly. They aim at different ways of knowing entirely. The method of science is an incomparable technique for the production of conscious, discursive knowledge, of descriptions of appearances. Its self-critical tradition, its careful definition of presuppositions and limits, and its openness and insistence on repeatability all help assure us that the knowledge we arrive at through scientific inquiry is reliable. There is nothing else that can compete.

But science is no use if we long to inhabit reality in the flesh. Reality is not and can never be an object of knowledge; any claim to know something about it has to originate after we've already cut ourselves apart from the world. What we long to do is to live consciously in the real world, and this is a far more difficult task than most of us would suppose. None of our usual ways of thinking and action can help us.

Religious practice and religious teaching arise from that longing to live real lives, as the unknowable beings that we really are. When their proponents claim to give us information about reality, they are indeed offering bad science—though no more than any artist does—and we have every right to read their words as poetry instead of statements of fact. When they offer us techniques and instructions in the difficult art of self-transformation, though, they are true to their calling. Life is music, and religion above all helps us to hear that music and dance with it. Through all of human history, it has been religion that has shown us how to live our lives abundantly, as moments in the intricate and endless play of the divine. Through its visions and metaphors, countless generations have learned how to embrace both joy and horror and perfection and ruin, to live serenely with whatever befalls, and to undertake the tasks at hand with a light heart and compassionate energy.

Everything said in the name of religion is literally false, but religion remains the one activity through which we direct ourselves toward reality. We would be far poorer without it. A world that did not open to what it discloses might not even be recognizable as a human one. But there is no need to worry. Gods may live and die and rituals and doctrines change, but there is no chance that spiritual practice will vanish in the face of science and reason. Science is supremely useful, even inspiring, but religion is essential. That is why it's not going away.

Notes

1. David Hume, *A treatise on human nature: Being an attempt to introduce the experimental method of reasoning into moral subjects; and dialogues concerning natural religion*, 2.3.3.4, SBN 415.
2. I remember sitting through a teaching by a Tibetan lama that was so prosaic and literal that my ability to work within that rich and powerful set of practices was permanently damaged.
3. The great mathematician Kurt Gödel proved this about any consistent logical system.
4. This is far too complex and controversial a topic to be treated fully here. As a start, however, it should be clear that telling someone that their subjective experience is merely a product of brain activity does

not explain how a pattern of brain activity could have subjective content, let alone how subjectivity itself could emerge.

5. Sam Harris, *The moral landscape: How science can determine human values* (New York: Simon and Schuster, 2010).

6. Ludwig Wittgenstein, *Tractatus logico-philosophicus* 70, 6.371–72.

7. "Picasso speaks" (interview with Marius de Zayas), *The Arts* (New York), May 1923. The full quote is, "Art is a lie that makes us realize truth, at least the truth that is given us to understand."

8. Tellingly, Picasso is often misquoted as saying that art is a lie that *tells us the truth*.

9. The parallel with art is apt, as art as an autonomous practice branched off from religion only a few hundred years ago in Europe; it is not wholly misleading to see it as an attempt at achieving the ends of religious practice without the religion.

10. Deuteronomy 4:24.

11. G. S. Kirk, J. E. Raven, and M. Schofield, *The presocratic philosophers* (Cambridge: Cambridge University Press, 1983), 198.

12. Matthew 16:25.

13. I owe much in the following discussion to M. Gabriel and S. Žižek, *Mythology, madness, and laughter: Subjectivity in German idealism* (New York: Continuum, 2009), but the perspective metaphor is my own.

14. Although I take issue with many of Mark Johnston's claims in his recent *Saving God: Religion after idolatry* (Princeton, NJ: Princeton University Press, 2009), what I am talking about here is very close to his notion of "process panentheism."

15. Against that preference, one could argue, for example, that temporary suffering is less invidious when it is visited on self-conscious entities because they at least know that it will come to an end.

16. Aristotle's ethics is humanist in many respects, but it is neither individualist nor rights based.

17. Blaise Pascal, Pensées, § 233 (trans. W. F. Trotter), cited at http://plato.stanford.edu/entries/pascal-wager/#2.

18. This line is universally attributed to Ivan Karamazov in Dostoyevsky's novel *The brothers Karamazov*, but though Ivan indicates as much, he never actually says this, and the famous words do not appear in the text; see http://www.infidels.org/library/modern/features/2000/cortesi1.html.

19. Ernst Fürlinger, *The touch of Śakti: A study in non-dualistic Trika Śaiv-ism of Kashmir* (New Delhi: D. K. Printworld, 2009), 255.

20. This was Marx's question at the beginning of his career, and readers may note significant echoes of the early Marx in what follows. This important element in Marx's thought probably originates from the fusion of spirituality and politics in the idealist tradition, especially in the still underappreciated work of Fichte, which similarly underlies much of this book's argument.

21. This is a caricature of Isaiah Berlin's "negative freedom" but not too much of one.

22. Charles Darwin, *The autobiography of Charles Darwin 1809–1882. With the original omissions restored. Edited and with appendix and notes by his grand-daughter Nora Barlow.* (London: Collins, 1958), 90. He could accept human suffering because people might learn and grow from it, but Darwin saw no use of any sort in the suffering of other creatures.

23. "The consummation of the infinite End . . . consists merely in remov-ing the illusion which makes it seem yet unaccomplished"; G. W. F. Hegel, *Hegel's Logic, being Part One of the* Encyclopedia of the Philo-sophical Sciences, trans. W. Wallace. (1873; reprint, Oxford: Claren-don Press, 1973), § 212, 274.

24. Jay L. Garfield, trans., *The fundamental wisdom of the middle way: Nāgārjuna's Mūlamadhyamakakārikā* (Oxford: Oxford University Press, 1995), 75, XXV: 19.

25. Johann Gottlieb Fichte, *The vocation of man*, trans. William Smith (Indianapolis: Bobbs-Merrill, 1956), 151.

Index

About the Author

Michael Steinberg is an independent scholar and attorney living in Rochester, New York. The author of *The Fiction of a Thinkable World: Body, Meaning, and the Culture of Capitalism* (Monthly Review Press, 2005), and *In the Land of Temples: Notes from a South Indian Pilgrimage* (KDP, 2012), he has published scholarly work in history, philosophy, music, and law and taught university-level courses in intellectual history; his special focus is on the eighteenth century and the philosophy of German idealism. His scholarly work is complemented by Steinberg's practice at a major center for South Indian tantrism, and his work seeks to bring a cross-cultural perspective to issues too often seen through Western eyes only.

Made in the USA
San Bernardino, CA
28 April 2014